Nick Hornby's
High Fidelity

CONTINUUM CONTEMPORARIES

Also available in this series

Pat Barker's *Regeneration*, by Karin Westman
Kazuo Ishiguro's *The Remains of the Day*, by Adam Parkes
Carol Shields's *The Stone Diaries*, by Abby Werlock
J.K. Rowling's *Harry Potter Novels*, by Philip Nel
Jane Smiley's *A Thousand Acres*, by Susan Farrell
Barbara Kingsolver's *The Poisonwood Bible*, by Linda Wagner-Martin
Irvine Welsh's *Trainspotting*, by Robert Morace
Donna Tartt's *The Secret History*, by Tracy Hargreaves
Toni Morrison's *Paradise*, by Kelly Reames
Don DeLillo's *Underworld*, by John Duvall
Annie Proulx's *The Shipping News*, by AlikiVarvogli
Graham Swift's *Last Orders*, by Pamela Cooper
Haruki Murakami's *The Wind-up Bird Chronicle*, by Matthew Strecher
Ian Rankin's *Black and Blue*, by Gill Plain
Michael Ondaatje's *The English Patient*, by John Bolland
Bret Easton Ellis's *American Psycho*, by Julian Murphet
Cormac McCarthy's *All the Pretty Horses*, by Stephen Tatum
Iain Banks's *Complicity*, by Cairns Craig
A.S. Byatt's *Possession*, by Catherine Burgass
David Guterson's *Snow Falling on Cedars*, by Jennifer Haytock
Helen Fielding's *Bridget Jones's Diary*, by Imelda Whelehan
Sebastian Faulks's *Birdsong*, by Pat Wheeler
Kate Atkinson's *Behind the Scenes at the Museum*, by Emma Parker
Hanif Kureishi's *The Buddha of Suburbia*, by Nahem Yousaf
Zadie Smith's *White Teeth*, by Claire Squires
Arundhati Roy's *The God of Small Things*, by Julie Mullaney
Alan Warner's *Morvern Callar*, by Sophy Dale
Vikram Seth's *A Suitable Boy*, by Angela Atkins
Margaret Atwood's *Alias Grace*, by Gina Wisker

Forthcoming in this series:

Jonathan Coe's *What a Carve Up!*, by Pamela Thurschwell
Louis De Bernieres's *Captain Corelli's Mandolin*, by Con Coroneos

NICK HORNBY'S

High Fidelity

A READER'S GUIDE

JOANNE KNOWLES

CONTINUUM | NEW YORK | LONDON

2002

The Continuum International Publishing Group Inc
370 Lexington Avenue, New York, NY 10017

The Continuum International Publishing Group Ltd
The Tower Building, 11 York Road, London SE1 7NX

www.continuumbooks.com

Printed in the United States of America

Library of Congress Catalog Card Number 2002 141141

ISBN 0-8264-5325-2

Contents

Acknowledgements

I would like to thank my parents Lucy and Arthur, and my husband Russ Glennon, for their support during the writing of this book. David Barker, my editor at Continuum, also deserves thanks for his patience and support, as does Nick Hornby for his helpfulness and generosity in contributing information.

The Novelist

In less than ten years, Nick Hornby has achieved huge success as a writer, both in fiction and non-fiction, and as a "literary" novelist as well as a best-selling one. This book is intended to guide readers towards some of the important and interesting facets of his first novel, *High Fidelity*, and through this provide a general understanding of Hornby's work. It begins with an overview of Hornby's career to date, putting *High Fidelity* into its cultural context before examining it more closely.

BIOGRAPHY

Nick Hornby was born in 1957 in Maidenhead, a suburban town southwest of London. His parents separated in 1968, and Hornby and his younger sister Gill (who would later marry the novelist Robert Harris, author of *Enigma, Fatherland*, and *Archangel* among other best-sellers) continued to live with their mother in Maidenhead, where Hornby attended Maidenhead Grammar School.

Hornby's father, who later remarried and had two more children, began to take his eleven-year-old son to football matches during his access visits, engendering the lifelong devotion to Arsenal, the North London football club, which is documented in *Fever Pitch*. This childhood was, while not being dramatically unhappy, certainly turbulent; Hornby was not popular at school, and his developing love of football can be seen as both a bonding experience with his father and as a way of carving an identity for himself which would steer him through the troubles of approaching adolescence.

Even though told through the lens of his obsession with football, *Fever Pitch* provides the reading public with a good autobiographical view of Hornby's life. It is inevitably weighted towards his childhood and youth and skims over the genesis of his writing career, perhaps the greatest loss to students of his novels. What it does best is to flesh out the bare facts and dates of Hornby's life with the same dry humor that characterizes his novels. While it would be rash to read all of his fictions in an autobiographical light on the basis of what we are told in *Fever Pitch*, it gives some clear indications of how Hornby's own experiences have served as inspiration for the concerns which dominate his fiction. The statements he makes about his own aimlessness are reminiscent of his fictions:

> I was still at school in 1975, but only just. I took my A levels that summer, and scraped by in two of the three subjects, and then, with breathtaking cheek, I decided to stay on for an extra term to study for the Cambridge entrance examinations—not, I think, because I wanted to go to Cambridge, but because I didn't want to go to university immediately, and yet neither did I want to travel round the world, or teach handicapped children, or work on a kibbutz, or do anything at all that might make me a more interesting person. (*Fever Pitch*, p. 86)

This kind of inertia is chronicled in the same way when Hornby writes about Rob Fleming or Will Freeman, similar to his own younger self in wanting to remain in the arena of adolescence where life choices and personal development are something to be avoided. Hornby goes on to describe how this adolescence is further prolonged by his taking a job with an insurance firm in London while he waits to hear about a university place. His aim was, at least partly, "to take my fascination with London to some kind of conclusion by becoming part of the place" (p. 92). However, as he says, Hornby remained an outsider, commuting in to work and having little contact with actual Londoners—though since these were deemed to be "people who lived in Gillespie Road, Avenell Road or Highbury Hill, N5, they were always going to be elusive" (p. 92). This failed quest for the authentic metropolitan experience is, again, reflected in many of Rob's remarks in *High Fidelity*, and, in a broader sense, explains Hornby's decision to locate his fictions in the North London he now knows. Like Jane Austen, he carefully chooses fictional territory with which he is familiar; however, his claim on North London is that of the convert or the expatriate rather than the native.

Cambridge was also a place where Hornby considered himself an outsider—he describes it as "awful." He has since discussed his naïve attempts to claim a kind of working-class identity for himself during his time there, adopting a stronger London accent and consciously developing a taste for Rod Stewart as a way of demonstrating his allegiance to the downmarket and anti-intellectual side of popular culture. His love of football remained constant, though he transferred his day-to-day support to the local team, Cambridge United, who, since they are in the second division of the British football league, cannot be seen as rivals to his "first team", Arsenal.

Having left university, Hornby took up a job as a garage mechanic before entering teacher training in 1980. He states that he "had no ambitions for myself before I was twenty-six or twenty-seven, when I decided that I could and would write for a living, packed my job in and waited around for publishers and/or Hollywood producers to call me up and ask me to do something for them sight unseen." (p. 111). In hindsight, this makes his teaching career seem like merely the prelude to his later role as a writer, and certainly there have been times, such as the one above, where he thought that way. However, his time as a teacher is also a strong influence on the kind of writer he has become and on the content of his novels. He said, during a reading in 2000, that he keeps diaries from his years as a teacher from which he draws inspiration, and that these even include registers of children's names, which he uses for minor characters in the novels. Marcus in *About A Boy* is, he has said, a direct product of his experiences teaching "alienated kids," specifically in Cambridge where pupils tended to come from a variety of international and social backgrounds. Given his consistent attention to the thin line which can divide childhood from maturity, his work as someone who oversees and supposedly encourages the growing-up process has fueled much of his fiction.

Hornby gave up his school teacher's post in favor of becoming a writer in 1983, yet he did not actually leave the world of education for some time. He moved back to London and took a job as a teacher of English as a foreign language, a "temporary job which somehow lasted four years" (p. 154). This was followed by a post with a Far Eastern trading company, officially as a teacher, but which developed into a range of duties broadly covering representation of the company in the UK to other British people and cultural translation of aspects of British life to his employers. At the beginning of 1989 he moved into a road near to the Arsenal ground, fulfilling a long-held dream, and finally taking up residence as a North Londoner.

Hornby's career as a writer took some time to get off the ground. He wrote book reviews for various publications, including *The Listener* and *Sunday Correspondent*, both of which subsequently folded. This work was hardly remunerative or secure, but editors recognized Hornby's talent and wanted to encourage it as best they could by giving him work. He sold his first piece of fiction to BBC Radio Four's "Morning Story" in 1989, but he continued scraping a living by occasional publications until his big break came several years later. He also wrote an academic study of contemporary American writers, which included his favorite novelist, Anne Tyler, and this was published by Vision Press in 1992.

In the summer of 1991, Hornby began writing *Fever Pitch*. It was championed by Liz Knights, editorial director at Victor Gollancz, and was published in 1992 with the hope that football fans would buy enough copies to justify its appearance. Word-of-mouth engendered unanticipated success for the book, which went on to sell 300,000 copies. It garnered popular and critical acclaim as a sports book, winning the William Hill Sports Book of the Year award, and also as a minor classic in the fields of comic and autobiographical writing. This was the beginning of a mutually profitable relationship with Gollancz, who were to publish Hornby's next two books before he signed a £2 million contract to move to Penguin Books in early 1999. *High Fidelity*, his first novel, was published in 1995 and followed by his second, *About a Boy*, in 1998, both receiving critical praise and achieving best-seller status.

Hornby married Virgina Bovell in 1993, and their son Danny was born in the same year. However, the marriage was quickly put under severe strain when Danny was diagnosed as autistic while still a toddler. The pressures of the situation resulted in the couple's split in 1998 and divorce in 2000, although they speak daily and share much of the responsibility for Danny. In 2000 *Speaking with the Angel*, an anthology of short fiction written in the first person and edited by Hornby, was published with the aim of raising funds for Treehouse, a special school for autistic children co-founded by Hornby and Danny's mother, along with several other parents in the same position. Some of the profits from the film adaptation of *About a Boy,* and from Hornby's 1999 publishing contract with Penguin, have also been earmarked for Treehouse funding.

Hornby's most recent novel, *How To Be Good,* was published in the spring of 2001. His next project, he has said, will be a screenplay he is co-writing with actress and filmmaker Emma Thompson. He has also written the introductions to the new Penguin editions of two P. G. Wodehouse novels, *Heavy Weather* and *Summer Lightning,* which will be available shortly. Other future plans are to write what he has described as "a little book about songs" before beginning on a new novel, possibly in the autumn of 2002.

HORNBY'S INFLUENCES: AUTHORS AND GENRES

In the spirit of *High Fidelity,* Hornby lists his top five writers as follows: Charles Dickens, Anne Tyler, Evelyn Waugh, P. G. Wodehouse, and Roddy Doyle. He has mentioned on a number of occasions his love of American literature, and his aspiration as a young writer to produce works like those of his favorite modern American novelists—Anne Tyler and Lorrie Moore among them. It might seem odd that only one American, Tyler, is in the list. However, two things should be borne in mind. First, the lesson to be learned from *High Fidelity* is that a top five list is always subject to change and to the mood of the day. Second, this list tells us a lot about Hornby's preferences in fiction, in terms of genre and style. All of the above are known for being both comic writers and to portraying social realism, often associated with a particular part of the world. Dickens's London, Tyler's Baltimore, and Doyle's Barrytown in Dublin are all tremendously important to their novels, in the way that the milieu of North London is to Hornby's own work, without reducing any of those novels to being simply about life in

London, Baltimore, or Dublin. Furthermore, the combination of comedy and social realism favored by these authors is perhaps the most important aim of Hornby's own novels.

REALISM, COMEDY AND DOMESTIC FICTION

When asked in interview, "What do you think is the purpose of fiction?", this was Hornby's reply:

> First and foremost to entertain. But what I mean by entertainment is really the affecting of the emotions in some way. Making people laugh, that to me is something that has always been amiss in literary fiction, that making people laugh is regarded as somehow not an important job. I think it is.

These comments demonstrate the position Hornby covets in the market for fiction. If a novelist is primarily a producer of entertainment, then the popularity of Hornby's novels proves his success in achieving his aims. However, they go beyond this: in discussing comedy as something that is often undervalued in "literary fiction," Hornby declares his aspiration to be not only a comic writer, but a literary one. Comedy is, as he says, often seen as a barrier to novels being regarded as "serious" and literary, yet the tradition of the realist novel allows for evoking laughter as well as profundity, as Dickens shows. In defining entertainment more broadly as "the affecting of the emotions in some way," Hornby aligns himself more closely with present-day peers in the straightforward popular fiction market, and with antecedents such as Dickens, than with his current "literary" peers, who are more likely to use irony and a postmodern mix of styles to keep readers at a distance.

Hornby carries this interest in "affecting the emotions" further, addressing gendered stereotypes of the kind of books that interest men and women respectively. Considering that he is often identified as very much a man's writer, his actual views on gendered reading are surprising and refreshing. He states:

> I usually read books by women and that's because I prefer books about the domestic, you know, that thing about recognition and the way you live your life. I wanted to try and write a kind of male equivalent of some of the best female novelists—there didn't seem to be stuff about what went on in ordinary guys' heads. If that's what I've done, I'm happy about that.

There are a number of ways in which Hornby belies his characterization as a novelist who defines and is defined by contemporary masculinity. One of these is, as he says above, his desire to write "domestic" fiction, the kind of novels supposedly written about women's interests, love, relationships, and life's everyday difficulties. Another is in his use of a "confessional" style, writing *High Fidelity* in the first person, as a painful, confession narrative where the central protagonist chronicled his own failures and problems. Similarly intimate fictional styles, such as the diary or memoir, are more often associated with female than with male writers (as can be seen by the recent success of Helen Fielding's *Bridget Jones's Diary*). He also uses the formulation—again, often characterized as feminine—of showing a protagonist's initial miseducation in the ways of life through studying fictional texts. Jane Austen's Catherine Morland in *Northanger Abbey* (1818) and the eponymous heroine of Gustave Flaubert's *Madame Bovary* (1857) are examples of heroines who are led astray by reading fiction and mistaking it for a faithful representation of real life. Hornby's Rob Fleming makes the same mistake, following a similar structure of miseducation, except that the insidious influence of fiction is replaced by one of its twentieth-century counterparts, pop music.

In spite of this, Hornby continues to be acclaimed as *the* contemporary chronicler of the male psyche—a label that is, like all such labels, reductive while containing a strong element of the truth. The background to this label is the instability, particularly with regard to men and their role in contemporary society, which characterized the early and mid 1990s, and is worth examining more closely as the conclusion to a survey of Hornby's work.

HORNBY AND MASCULINITY IN CRISIS

If every cultural movement begins as a rebellion against its predecessor, then images of masculinity in the early 1990s have to be considered as a backlash against those which dominated the 1980s. During that decade the "New Man" gained popularity, representing a progressive model for masculinity as someone who would share housework and other "feminine" tasks, who was in touch with his feelings, and who regarded women as partners and equals. In opposition to this, the image of the "Lad" or "New Lad" arose in the early 1990s as a generally middle-class figure espousing attitudes and behaviors conventionally (though not necessarily correctly) attributed to the working classes. Lads took up an anti-intellectual position, scorning sensitivity and caring in favor of drinking, violence, and a pre-feminist attitude to women as both sex objects and creatures from another species. They promoted un-PC views and a hedonistic attitude to life, scorning ideas of career aspiration or "settling down" for an uproarious social life with their friends and casual relationships with women. These attitudes were often claimed to be held "ironically," but they nevertheless entered mainstream culture, where they were promoted as a model for 1990s masculinity.

Various opinions exist as to what motivated this shift in gender politics. It was at least partly generated by the enthusiasm of the media: the British magazine *Loaded*, which was launched in 1993 and became a kind of style guide for New Lads, was at one time credited with single-handedly creating Lad culture. On the other hand, it was considered to be a product of genuine social instability. The idea that men could suddenly be regarded as an oppressed group might seem implausible. Nevertheless, as various stories emerged about the erosion of traditional male employment in manufacturing and other industries, the academic underachievement of boys, and the improved accessibility of careers and independent lives for women, a persuasive case was built to support the idea that masculinity was in crisis.

Ian Miles catalogued these developments in 1989, warning of a resurgence of conservative feeling if they were not addressed: "It seems likely than many of the structural changes that underpin the crisis of masculinity will continue their evolution. [. . . .] For these and other reasons, the traditional forms of masculinity are likely to be continually placed in crisis. It is hard to assess what political results this might have in a post-New Right scenario. [. . . .] What can be forecast is that the stresses and strains discussed above will not go away, and that many of them are likely to intensify" (Miles, p. 55).

As a result, the rise of the New Lad coincided with a backlash against feminism by both women and men, as documented by Susan Faludi's *Backlash*. With hindsight, it can be seen more easily that many of the factors which created the masculinity crisis were based on class and economics, rather than gender, and so it was far from being a universal phenomenon. Lynne Segal observes that:

> The most significant differences on display are differences between men themselves, rather than between men and women. Thus it is particular groups of men, especially unemployed, unskilled and unmarried, who have

far higher mortality and illness rates compared with other groups of men. (Segal, xi)

However, this message was largely ignored in favor of a more media-friendly image of the battle of the sexes. At the height of New Laddism, male-female relationships were popularly portrayed as being defined by the title of John Gray's self-help best-seller, *Men Are From Mars, Women Are From Venus* (1993). On its appearance, *High Fidelity* was hailed as a definitive guide to the crisis of the contemporary male and on the difficulty of Nineties Man (or Lad) in relating successfully to women. An outline of the novel can give the impression that Rob represents the archetypal New Lad, and this was accentuated by the fact that *Fever Pitch* had already been adopted as a guiding text for the football-fixated Lad. However, the novel actually paints a more complex picture of masculinity than it is commonly perceived to do. The following section of the guide, which examines the main themes of *High Fidelity*, will look at its portrayals of masculinity, realism, and other factors such as the consumption of pop music as key issues in the novel.

SUMMARY

Hornby's fiction deals with questions about where meaning might be found in life, as well as where a girlfriend might be found, and therefore goes beyond the aspirations of much popular fiction. It also deals with where meaning might be found in *texts*, showing the two to be interdependent, and thus demonstrating good postmodern credentials. The novel draws on traditional literary elements as well as more contemporary and skeptical ones, accommodating both these strands through the medium of popular fiction, and through a plot framework which can accommodate traditional notions of character progress, popular notions of romance, and postmodern notions of commodification and skeptical materialism.

High Fidelity's various structural and plot elements, then, demonstrate the evolution of how a realistic novel can have been said to work at various times from the nineteenth century to the present day and what values and techniques become assimilated into the form. Hornby's work shares many of the ideals of the high realist period, while being only too aware of the modernist and postmodern views that have subsequently undermined the realist approach to representation and its view of the world as displayed in fiction. All this is worn lightly, but nevertheless his novels—and *High Fidelity* in particular—are very much the product of over a century's worth of literary debate over what a novel, and by implication what a life, should be about, and where its meaning may be found.

2

The Novel

There are a number of major issues to be considered when examining *High Fidelity*, which belong to two equally important fields of enquiry. First, its *literary* properties, including its influences, structure, narrative technique, and the genre to which it belongs. Second, its presentation of *social* and *cultural* values. This section of the book will survey the issues and themes which are important in *High Fidelity* in relation to those areas. It is divided into five sections. In the first I look at *High Fidelity* as part of a specific genre within the realist novel: the *bildungsroman*. Third, I examine the impact of place and provinciality in the novel. The third section examines masculinity and the "crisis of masculinity" as portrayed in the novel. Fourth, I explore the novel's presentation of pop music and its influence. The final section, following on from this consideration of popular culture, investigates postmodernism and its presence in *High Fidelity*.

HIGH FIDELITY AS *BILDUNGSROMAN*, OR NOVEL OF DEVELOPMENT

The *bildungsroman* is a particular genre of novel that enjoyed its heyday during the nineteenth century, when the popularity of the novel as a form, and realism as a fictional method, were also at their height. Originally a German concept, and deriving from the example set by Goethe's *Wilhelm Meister's Apprenticeship* (1795–6), it is usually translated as "novel of development," "novel of education," or "formation novel" and became popular in England as a form during the great age of the Victorian novel. It has been summarized by Chris Baldick as follows: "A kind of novel that follows the hero or heroine from childhood or adolescence into adulthood, through a troubled quest for identity [. . . .] Many outstanding novels of the nineteenth and early twentieth centuries follow this pattern of personal growth." (Baldick, p. 30) This conveys some of the feeling that as a *literary* form, this model has been discarded since the days of high modernism. Indeed, the rise of postmodernism marks the adoption of literary and cultural values that are in many ways directly opposed to the values of *bildungsroman*—I'll discuss this potential opposition more in the section on postmodernism later.

The common pattern of the *bildungsroman* can be seen in well-known examples such as Charles Dickens's *David Copperfield* (1850) or Charlotte Brönte's *Jane Eyre* (1847). The typical *bildungsroman* hero, like David Copperfield, strays from the down-to-earth values of his upbringing into jobs and relationships which are unsuitable for him before undergoing a moral or spiritual awakening that teaches him how he should be spending his life. He (for various reasons, the hero is usually male) can then take up his true vocation and find his soulmate, often then achieving worldly and financial success as a result of, and reward for, his realizations. Thus David

Copperfield eventually becomes a writer and, after an immature marriage, settles down with the wise and virtuous Agnes, while Jane Eyre is rewarded for her moral fortitude by receiving an inheritance and being allowed to marry Mr. Rochester after the convenient death of his first wife. As the golden age of realism receded toward the end of the nineteenth century, to be replaced first by *fin-de-siecle* fears of degeneration in society, and then the rise of modernism, the *bildungsroman*, with its focus on bringing the individual's aspirations in line with their community's social and moral standards, lost favor as a literary form. While realist novels focusing on the development of the individual continued to be written, they were superseded in the literary views of the twentieth century by more avant-garde forms of narrative, such as James Joyce's *Portrait of the Artist as a Young Man* (1916), a distinctly modern *bildungsroman* which uses a self-consciously difficult range of narrative styles and voices. The hero, Stephen Dedalus, finally leaves his community to develop himself rather than learning to place himself within it as his nineteenth-century predecessors did. The lingering influence of modernism can be seen in the fact that a novel written in a realist format is, even at the beginning of the twenty-first century, likely to be considered less literary than one with a more experimental and fragmented form. Nevertheless, popular fiction generally follows this form and is very successful in doing so. This section looks at Hornby's use of the *bildungsroman* model and, in doing so, at how he bridges the gap between popular realism and a more literary self-awareness and postmodern outlook. In this way, the tradition to which Hornby is indebted can be examined before subsequently turning to his points of departure from this tradition.

A number of critical works on the *bildungsroman* have been produced, the most useful being by Jerome Buckley and Franco Moretti. They show that the typical *bildungsroman* protagonist eventually recognizes and acquires the following qualities:

- The right partner (inevitably a heterosexual, prospective marital partner)
- A work ethic, resulting in a rewarding occupation or career
- A meaningful and respectful relation to their roots, community, and family
- Some form of spiritual fulfilment, even if in a secular context

At the beginning of *High Fidelity*, Rob Fleming lacks most of these qualities only possessing a kind of spiritual practice in his devotion to music. The novel shows his education in learning the relative worth of these other goals and aspiring towards a life in which all of them are balanced. In spite of his many contemporary habits and tastes, Rob sees himself as having fallen foul of the traditional distraction from the path of achievements in life: the wrong woman. Reflecting on his relationship with Charlie Nicholson, he compiles the following set of rules for guidance: "Here's how not to plan a career: a) split up with girlfriend; b) junk college; c) go to work in record shop; d) stay in record shops for rest of life" (p. 27).

Rob maintains that his career, as owner and manager of a record store, wasn't the result of choice but "a few short weeks in 1979 when I went potty for a while" (p. 27). The implication is that career decisions should be made after careful thought, should involve as much formal education as possible, and certainly shouldn't be made on the basis of romantic entanglements (or, to be more specific, in the aftermath of romantic disasters). However, Rob is part of a fictional tradition where one's youth is spent doing the wrong job and being with the wrong partner, before maturity brings you to your senses and puts you in a position to choose more wisely. Although Rob is thirty-five, becoming thirty-six during the course of the novel, he is clearly still going through the *bildungsroman* process. After a conversation about Dick's new girlfriend in which it becomes clear that Barry is jealous, Rob says:

> I feel as though I have been having conversations like this all my life. None of us is young any more, but what has just taken place could have happened when I was sixteen, or twenty, or twenty-five. We got to adolescence and just stopped dead; we drew up the map then and left the boundaries exactly as they were. (p. 125)

Rob's adolescence has been considerably prolonged, but his experiences during the novel are clearly recognizable as part of the journey towards adulthood and maturity. Rob himself is only partially aware of this to begin with, and even when he recognizes it, still has some way to go before he stops resisting this recognition and acts upon it. After meeting Marie LaSalle and feeling attracted to her not long after his break-up with Laura, he muses: "I hate all this stuff. How old do you have to get before it stops?" (p. 60).

The lesson Rob learns, in true *bildungsroman* style, is that one reaches maturity when one decides to act maturely. He grows up when he wants to do so—in fact, when he finally rejects the memory of his early romantic experiences with Charlie and others as things he no longer wants—and receives the traditional rewards of a stable relationship and a new (or renewed) vocation in life, in doing so.

Rob's role in the novel is, in part, to represent an Everyman character, typical both of the thirtysomething man in the late twentieth century and also of the universal man reaching maturity. Hornby skilfully draws attention to this through Rob's own articulation of his ordinariness:

> What am I? Average. A middleweight. Not the brightest bloke in the world, but certainly not the dimmest [. . . .] My genius, if I can call it that, is to

combine a whole load of averageness into one compact frame [. . . .] If I do OK with women, it's not because of the virtues I have, but because of the shadows I don't have. (pp. 29–30)

One of the shared qualities of most *bildungsroman* and most popular novels is the high priority given in the narrative to romantic fulfillment. Rob is no exception in finding this important. Unusually for a contemporary male protagonist, he openly articulates his desire for a partner as all-important, certainly to someone in his social circumstances, living an average Western urban lifestyle. He says:

It's only just beginning to occur to me that it's important to have something going on somewhere, at work or at home, otherwise you're just clinging on. If I lived in Bosnia, then having a girlfriend wouldn't seem like the most important thing in the world, but here in Crouch End it does. You need as much ballast as possible to stop you floating away. (p. 67)

This idea of surrounding yourself with "ballast" forms part of Rob's ideas about what constitutes a "real" life, something he doesn't think he has. The apparent flimsiness and transience of his existence are reduced, in his considerations of the subject, to two origins. They are his inability to believe in the permanence of any relationship, and his own dissatisfaction and embarrassment about his job, which feels more like a hobby, an adolescent distraction from the "real" facts of working life, such as making profits. At this point Rob recognizes the relativism of his position—if he were living in a war zone, his particular choice of reality would seem trivial—but as the novel, and his feelings about Laura, develops, this longing for a partner becomes a need that transcends all other considerations:

> This, really, is the bottom line, the chief attraction of the opposite sex for all of us, old and young, men and women; we need someone to save us from the sympathetic smiles in the Sunday night cinema queue, someone who can stop us from falling down into the pit where the permanently single live with their mums and dads. (p. 118)

The separation from parental authority is another part of growing up which features heavily in the *bildungsroman*, as does its counterpart, the finale in which the protagonist reconciles to some extent with his family and his unfashionable beginnings. It is significant then that Rob's reunion with Laura takes place in the context of her father's funeral, an occasion for mourning a parent, remembering a past life, and also marking the point at which a new one begins. In walking out of Ken's funeral wake, they enact a traditional detachment from parental values in order to make a more profound compact with one another.

However, the funeral scene demonstrates a number of aspects of the Rob-Laura dynamic. As at so many other points in the novel, it is Laura who not only becomes the catalyst for action but who acts while Rob makes decisions in the wake of hers. She is the one who pushes for progress and development in life and in their relationship, while Rob remains static. Tellingly, he states on meeting her again after she has left him: "She thinks she's started out on a new stage in her life. She hasn't. I'm not going to let her" (p. 126).

High Fidelity's debt to *bildungsroman* is a somewhat ironic one as highlighted by this statement. Some of this irony is deployed in the context of gender politics, and will be discussed more fully in the later section on masculinity. However, one of the structural ways in which it ironizes *bildungsroman* is by portraying Rob's main goal as being the delaying of the *bildungsroman* process. While other *bildungsroman* protagonists are often confused about the direction they wish to take and remain in an unproductive situation for some time, Rob is different in being actively concerned to arrest his own development and, therefore, that of others like Laura so that he isn't left behind. "New stages" in anyone's life only serve to retard his own status: he becomes shamefully aware of this when he sees the way Barry wants to spoil Dick's pleasure at having found a girlfriend, recognizing some of his own motives and being repelled by them. The factors which overcome this are connected with a fear of his own mortality, and a wish to dwell in the past while being detached from it. Rob eventually revisits the emotional landscape of his past, exorcising the power of his memories by placing them in a context of progression.

It is the act of imagining his past girlfriends in list form, as static beings, that must be laid to rest; seeing them as adult women, with lives, partners, and careers which have developed detaches him from them all, including Charlie. In a typical *bildungsroman*, a protagonist would meet an old flame again but realize that with their newly acquired maturity, their early infatuation with that person, seems ill-judged—as Pip does with Estella in Dickens's *Great Expectations*. While there is an element of this in Rob's experiences—most significantly in relation to Charlie, who is demystified and brought down to earth—it also happens in reverse. Because Penny Ellis, Jackie Allen, and his other teenage girlfriends have moved on, they are no longer interested in or available to him. More straightforwardly, Rob now has the opportunity to reject those who rejected him, while those he rejected get revenge in their own lack of interest in him. As a *bildungsroman* protagonist, Rob is surrounded by its qualities in other people so that his own narrative is essentially the story of how he loses his determination to *resist* the inevitable progress of life.

Having dismissed the options he believed had been kept open (in Laura's phrasing), Rob is brought to recognize his fear of commitment to one partner as a fear of their mortality and, by implication, his own. He represses this feeling for a long time, with statements like: "If people have to die, I don't want them dying near me. My mum and dad won't die near me, I've made bloody sure of that. When they go, I'll hardly feel a thing" (p. 184).

The logic that keeping a physical distance from his parents will prevent the pain of their loss is consciously false reasoning on Rob's part (after all, this has hardly been the case with Charlie Nicholson, as he knows only too well). Being forced to think about death when Laura's father dies, he is able to confront his real attitude to life:

> I saw, for the first time, how scared I am of dying, and of other people dying, and how this fear has prevented me from doing all sorts of things [. . .] thinking about my life, and especially my job, in a way that contains a concept of the future (too scary, because the future ends in death). But most of all it has prevented me sticking with a relationship [. . . .] If that sounds feeble and self-serving at the same time—oh, right! He sleeps with other women because he has a fear of death!—well, I'm sorry, but that's the way things are. (p. 196)

Rob's tone here is that of someone who wishes to mock his own resemblance to a Freudian psychological case, or to an example in a self-help book. Yet this statement is more productive than Rob's self-mockery suggests. His previous aversion to self-development no longer obstructs his progress in life after this moment of realization. While character integrity is maintained by Rob's tone here which continues to be as irreverent and self-mocking as it has been throughout, this admission of his own fear, in true self-development style, allows him to overcome it. Paradoxically, too, the ability to move on allows Rob to choose to stay exactly where he is: managing his record shop and in his relationship with Laura. This fulfills, however, one of the final requirements of a novel of self-development, which is for the protagonist to realize the worth of what they have possessed, or what has been within reach, all along. Humanist values are the cornerstone of the realistic novel and its morality; similarly, *High Fidelity* affirms that people are more important than music, but in the style of the nineteenth-century novel, rewards Rob for this assumption with a renewed enjoyment of the thing he was prepared to give up.

The spiritual dimension of a *bildungsroman* is, typically, not formally religious. Since its popularity as a form occurred in the age of Darwin, when writers were trying to reconcile diminishing faith in God with the continued need for a spiritual belief, the *bildungsroman* protagonist often discovers a need for "something more" in life which eventually draws them away from "false idols" of pleasure, such as excessive drinking and sexual activity. For Rob, "something more" has been music, which in fact has been everything, crowding out other areas of life. However, this begins to be replaced as he works through his list by the idea of the right partner as being the "something more" he seeks. This ideal of a partnership which would be more than sexual already holds, for Rob, an almost spiritual dimension. He muses midway through the novel on the attraction of "Women who seem to need the love of a good man—I could rescue them, redeem them" (p. 158). However, Rob reconciles sheer pleasure and spiritual satisfaction in the novel's conclusion. Having seen his obsession with music put into perspective, he is allowed to retain it having found that lifelong partnership—or at least a willingness to work at and aspire to it.

Again, in the manner of the now-developed hero, Rob realizes that this meaningful, potentially transcendental relationship with a woman—one which makes both their lives seem special and worthwhile, rather than ordinary and pointless—has been under his nose and in his possession all along in the shape of Laura. This represents another significant way in which *High Fidelity* acts as an ironic *bildungsroman*: it is Laura who saves Rob, who acts to give him the mature life he now aspires to and deserves. He has achieved self-development in understanding himself better, yet she actually carries out the next step of taking action by deciding to resume their relationship, saying "We're going home" (p. 205), and arranging for Rob's return to DJing. Rob does ask her to marry him, but even this provides an ironic twist in that it is an act which is typical of a *bildungsroman* finale and one which, in this contemporary form of the *bildungsroman*, is rejected. The nineteenth-century ideal and structure of progressing towards self-development is given fresh life in *High Fidelity*, even though the context in which it happens is very different.

PLACE, PROVINCIALITY AND THE MIDDLE CLASSES

Rob's Everyman status is both highlighted and restricted by his own consciousness of his British suburban roots. He is quick to disclaim any interesting or individual features for his home and family. "I could have lived in any suburb in England—it was that sort of suburb, and that sort of park" (p. 9). This is specific even in its generality, though; it relies on a reader who does identify with this particularly anonymous slice of British urban life. Familiarity breeds contempt, and Rob assumes that this contempt will be shared by his readers who will themselves have grown up with, and therefore despise, such provinciality. He aspires to the kind of coolness that truly urban living—in other words, living in a big city, which in Britain means London—confers.

There is a certain irony in Rob's complaint that his hometown is anonymous when what seems really desirable is the even greater anonymity of the city, where you can strip away social identity and create an entirely new persona for yourself. As Rob states: "By moving to London, I had made it easier to be liked by girls" (p. 24).

Coolness is attributed to the crowd of people who, like Charlie when Rob meets her, seem incredibly at home in the city and who seem to have emerged into the world as they are now, having avoided a process of growing up and having shed an embarrassing past.

To a certain extent, Rob is highly conscious of his own provinciality and self-deprecating about it. However, there are points in the novel where aspects of Rob's character come across as deeply rooted in provincial and middle-class prejudices, of which he (and perhaps Hornby) are unaware. For instance, he describes how:

> At about half-past eleven, an Irish drunk called Johnny stumbles in. He comes to see us about three times a week, and his visits have become choreographed and scripted routines neither he nor I would want to change. In a hostile and unpredictable world, we rely on each other to provide something to count on. (p. 41)

It seems more than usually arrogant of Rob to assume that Johnny would never want to expand on an exchange which invariably ends with him being thrown bodily back into the street where he sleeps. As with Rob's parents, Johnny is an uncomfortable figure for Rob, one he has to keep at arm's length because of the fear that he himself will turn into Johnny—the dividing line between them is too perilously thin and needs to be physically shored up by distance. I quoted earlier Rob's statement that he keeps his parents, and thus their eventual illness and death, well away from himself and his life. With Johnny, too, he wants to restrict his contract with this desperate and desolate man to the "choreographed and scripted routine" that also represents his phone calls to his parents, and, in fact, his interactions with anyone whom he fears that he may become like—Dick, for example, or his Smiths-obsessed young male customers. This fear generates the patronizing assumption that a homeless person does not have to be treated as a human being like Rob himself, as possessing desires, aspirations, or feelings that can be hurt. Rob fails to align himself with the "hostile and unpredictable world" that actually oppresses Johnny as part of a class who are affluent enough to take ownership (even when shored up by a girlfriend's financial support) for granted. Rob uses the middle-class language of acquisition when he states, in parenthesis, that: "I haven't let the grass grow under my feet the last fourteen years! About ten years ago I borrowed the money to start my own!" (p. 27). In spite of his resistance to many other trappings of respectability, Rob has (almost without noticing) succumbed to the pursuit of capital and the middle-class aspiration towards property ownership. Rob in fact represents one of the most conventional British figures possible: the shopkeeper and small businessman.

Just as Rob assumes he understands Johnny's feelings and desires, so he assumes that he has the full measure of his parents and their lives, something conveyed by his statement that: "Home home is near Watford—somewhere I know" (p. 113). Rob's parents are never allowed to become more than two-dimensional (except for the imagined response of his father in their conversation about sex). He says his parental home is "somewhere he knows," but he doesn't actually know it at all—his parents are unexpectedly out when he arrives, and the film they go and see, *Howard's End,* is not on their top-five all time favorite list, while they have forsaken the one that is, *Genevieve,* to go to a wine-tasting. Rob's parents are much more unpredictable than he thinks, but to acknowledge that would be to recognize that he himself resembles the caricatured view he has of *them* too closely for comfort.

Even at a relatively late stage in the novel, when Rob is revising many of his previous assumptions, his judgements on people in terms of their place of residence and social class remain prejudiced and unquestioned. On his way to Charlie's dinner party after they have re-established contact, he remarks that "Charlie lives in Ladbroke Grove, of course" (p. 151). This is a fairly culturally specific reference, relying on the reader knowing that Ladbroke Grove is an area of West London which, in the 1990s, balanced being fashionably upmarket with being a touch bohemian—thus housing the kind of comfortably off liberals that Rob despises and likes to think he has nothing in common with. It is in this sense that *High Fidelity* is, as well as being a provincial novel, also a London novel in the tradition of Dickens in which the cultural landscape from West London to the Seven Sisters Road (the location of Championship Vinyl) is mapped out according to the values of late twentieth-century urban living.

While not overtly a political novel, *High Fidelity* also alludes to the specific political atmosphere of the early 1990s in Britain. During this period a Conservative government was still in power, but without anyone quite believing how it had happened (the Conservatives retained power in 1992 with an extremely slim majority of 21 seats in the House of Commons) and with the grey, uncharismatic figure of John Major as Prime Minister. The mood of the nation, as captured in *High Fidelity*, is one of quiet deflation after the exuberant economic and consumer attitudes of the 1980s, reflected in the "bad patch" being experienced by Championship Vinyl. Property owning and entrepreneurship are no longer seen as an infallible ideal, as Rob finds out, and a number of world conflicts in which the UK is to participate—the Gulf War, the crisis in the former Yugoslavia—are either in process or on the horizon. Furthermore, some of the less munificent aspects of the legacy of the 1980s are firmly in place, one of those being the evolution of Laura's career from legal aid lawyer to hotshot City brief. Rob reports that "She had to take a job that paid about forty-five grand a year because she couldn't find one that paid under twenty—she said that this was all you needed to know about Thatcherism, and I suppose she had a point" (p. 78).

Rob is hardly politically active, yet he is aware that the changes in the political climate since his own personal heyday as a DJ during the late 1980s have had an effect even on unpoliticized lives like his own. Neither his job nor Laura's yield satisfaction in the way that they used to, and have given way to insecurity and a need to scrabble for survival. For Rob, the political is very much personal. His concern with the change in direction in Laura's career is motivated by her change towards him and the effect it has on his own self-confidence. Furthermore, the downturn in the economy which has resulted in Rob losing custom is mainly significant to him as a threat which might force him out of his musical cocoon and see him "go off to work in a Virgin Megastore" (p. 41). Charlie's dinner party incites him to reflect more overtly than usual on his own subdued feelings of cultural and class inferiority:

> I'm not a class warrior [. . . .] Do I want some of what they've got? You bet. I want their opinions, I want their money, I want their clothes, I want their ability to talk about dogs' names without any hint of embarrassment. I want to go back to 1979 and start all over again. (p. 160)

Rob turns out to be an aspiring middle-class businessman after all, wanting to move on upwards to a level of self-assurance that he also despises. There is no need in his world for a radical restructuring of class boundaries, since that would remove his position within the sardonic minority. In the same way, it would not be desirable for the record-buying public to develop, *en masse*, a taste for Al Green and Elvis Costello, since the specialisms of Championship Vinyl staff would then become merely mainstream. What he actually wants is for his fellow dinner guests *not* to have these advantages, just as he does not want Laura to move on; his aspirations are chiefly negative. His satisfaction is found in asserting that he doesn't want to be like the people who have material things, unless those things are admirable records—possessions which, as in the case of the collector who left his wife for a new young girlfriend, override all other moral considerations.

Middle-class sensibility is something Rob enjoys sneering at, in the form of people who buy middle-of-the-road rock and jazz or who really like Elton John, but which he also feels uncomfortable being without—as in his discomfort that Laura earns more than he does, and that he may be looked down upon by "proper" working men. For the same reason, he sneers at those who have themselves departed from, and are denying, their middle-class origins: those who live in "Ladbroke Grove, of course," implying parental-style disapproval in the phrase "of course." The fact is, redemption is possible for Rob and for Barry, both middle-class men who lose their way. For those below or above them in the social framework, such as Johnny or Charlie, there is no such opportunity within the novel. Hornby is not concerned here with the possibilities of finding a vocation which lies outside this social sphere. However, his next novel, *About A Boy*, continues some of these themes while considering the question of what life might be like without the need to work, and where, in that event, meaning might be found.

Typically for Rob, music provides the best analogy for the tangle of social and class-based assumptions that have taken his life in its current direction: "In Bruce Springsteen songs, you can either stay and rot, or you can escape and burn [. . . .] You can leave the suburbs for the city and end up living a suburban life anyway" (pp. 113–4). This suggests a dawning consciousness that life is more complex than its encapsulation in a pop song. However, Rob still sees it the other way round: the pop song is an ideal he has failed to live up to in his own life.

High Fidelity is most susceptible to criticism on terms of class assumptions and prejudices; more so than on the grounds of its portrayal of gender roles or even the worth of music and popular culture. These assumptions remain firmly rooted at the end of the novel. Rob does not discover any need to change them, to rethink his feelings about Laura's job in the way that he does about her lawyer colleague Paul and his wife, Miranda. This may be an area in which Hornby's own complex feelings about his suburban home in Maidenhead, and the North London life he coveted as a teenager, are given less scrutiny than the other personal interests (in this instance, pop music) which provide material for his work. As a result, then, while there is a genuine "universalism" to be appreciated in *High Fidelity*, the geographical and social details of the cultural sphere it describes should not be assumed to represent the "average" qualities that Rob finds in himself.

MASCULINITY

For many readers, masculinity is what *High Fidelity* is all about. Since *Fever Pitch*'s success, Hornby has been associated with images of the "New Lad," and, more broadly, with ideas of what men should be like which formed part of the so-called "backlash" against feminism that gained popularity during the 1990s. I discussed in the first chapter of the book the concept of "masculinity in crisis" as one often thought to be exemplified by *High Fidelity*. In this section I will examine how this apparent masculinity crisis is diagnosed and treated in *High Fidelity*.

My earlier discussion of *bildungsroman* noted the irony of Laura's role as the active protagonist, in contrast to Rob's passivity. In fact, *High Fidelity* is a novel full of active and initiative-taking women (Laura, Marie LaSalle, Liz) in contrast to unassuming and mild-mannered men—even T-Bone is "a really nice guy" (p. 82). Conventional models of male success who are ruthless and forthright are notably lacking in this novel. For all its talk of laddishness and use of a lad's vocabulary and attitudes, these attitudes rarely translate into actions. Theoretical, rather than actual, laddism is the domain of Rob, Dick, and Barry—as seen by their acceptance, however reluctant, of Anna, Dick's new girlfriend, into the fold, and by Barry's capitulation to playing popular material instead of the planned repertoire of Sonic Death Monkey.

It is useful to examine one extended instance of Rob's feelings about gender relations and about the increasingly victimized role of men in the contemporary world in order to explore some of the genuine appeal of this view, and also some of its less agreeable exaggerations. This passage occurs early on in the novel, in the first section titled "Then," a retrospective on Rob's youthful relationships:

> Men—those little boys ten or twenty or thirty years on—are hopeless in bed. They are not interested in "foreplay" [. . . .] These complaints, you can't help feeling, are kind of ironic. Back then, all we wanted was foreplay, and girls weren't interested [. . . .] It's really not very surprising, then, that we're not much good at it. We spent two or three long and extremely formative years being told not even to think about it. Between the ages of fourteen and twenty-four, foreplay changes from something that boys want to do and girls don't, to something women want and men can't be bothered with [. . . .] The perfect match, if you ask me, is between the Cosmo woman and the fourteen-year-old boy. (p. 16)

This argument is carried off with some bravado, and is one of many such passages that have earned *High Fidelity* its reputation as a manifesto in defense of the Lad. It positions men as a group bewildered, and even repressed, by the behavioral norms imposed by girls on their teenage dating rituals, and in a wider sense, baffled by the cultural authorities who establish these standards, which make no sense in the light of women's more mature sexual requirements. Rob's argument is actually derived in a large part from his own immaturity here. Why *should* women, or men, want the same things at fourteen as they do at twenty-four? His own extended adolescence prevents him from acknowledging the necessity, and even desirability, of one's objectives, sexual or otherwise, changing in the years between adolescence and adulthood. Moreover, the original placing of "foreplay" in quotation marks reveals the truth of Rob's attitude towards it. He and his teenage peers did not conceptualize what they wanted to do as foreplay, just as something which would give them satisfaction (in the context of how impressed their peer group would be) rather than an act which primarily focused on the girls. The image of teenage boys as inherently concerned with altruistically dispensing sexual pleasure is a rather tongue-in-cheek justification of the subsequent attitude of "See! You've only got yourselves to blame!" The dismissal, too, of female teenagers as "not interested" in foreplay moves the argument into a rather one-sided territory—where cultural pressure and youthful repressive experiences are allowed to explain confused responses and poor performance on the part of men, without extending the same courtesy to women. Penny Hardwick, for example, might have bowed to social expectations, parental orders, or peer pressures to resist Rob's sexual advances as she did. For men to be portrayed as misunderstood is one thing; for them to occupy the position of victimized group is quite another, and therefore Rob's promotion of the male cause can frequently, as in this instance, cross the line between redressing the balance and demanding special and indeed unmerited advantages.

However, the point that the emotional needs of men have been too easily stereotyped is one to which *High Fidelity* draws justified attention, even though some of the conclusions provided by the novel may not be as flattering as advocates of Lad culture might like. I discussed earlier the caricatures of New Man and Lad which were established as opposites in the 1990s. The difficulty explored by *High Fidelity* is that these extremes seem to be the only received models for contemporary masculinity, with very little interest in representations of the middle ground. Rob frequently displays Lad aspirations, which can turn into Lad tendencies. Both this and the New Man model become, as we shall see, images he wishes at various times to emulate rather than stereotypes which he consistently fulfils.

The essential image of the Lad can be located in a number of images Rob constructs, which idealize the man who projects an apathetic, emotionless persona:

> There are men who call, and men who don't call, and I'd much, much rather be one of the latter. They are *proper* men, the sort of men that women have in mind when they moan about us. It's a safe, solid, meaningless stereotype: the man who appears not to give a shit. (p. 129)

This is emphasized by other remarks like this one, referring to Dick and Barry:

> I never remember their birthdays—you don't, do you, unless you are of the female persuasion? (p. 170)

Beyond this, there is the strategy of employing emotional rhetoric for manipulative purposes. When Liz accuses him of being the kind of man unable to say, "I love you," Rob thinks: "Those men don't exist. Saying 'I love you' is easy, a piece of piss, and almost every man I know does it all the time. I've *acted* as though I haven't been able to say it a couple of times" (p. 134).

In contrast to all this, there is the image of the New Man functioning as a polar opposite, especially in the all-important arena of relationships with women. The image is invoked ironically—again as a standard too hopelessly high to be consistently met—when Rob begins a short-lived relationship with Marie LaSalle: "I feel like a new man, although not very much like a New Man. I feel so much better, in fact, that I go straight out and sleep with Marie" (p. 95).

The New Man seems, by this inference, to be an unreachable ideal who does exactly the opposite of the average, red-blooded male—one who has subjugated his own masculinity in order to fulfill the needs of women. However, this passive and insipid image is superseded by the entrance of a "real" New Man into the narrative, who visits Championship Vinyl to buy his wife a birthday present:

> He's well-spoken, and he's wearing a suit, and he's dangling his car keys and for some reason these things make me feel maybe two decades younger than him, twenty or so to his fortysomething. I have this burning desire to find out what he thinks of me [. . . .] I'm patently not a grown-up man in a grown-up job (p. 137)

This image of the New Man in his suit seems to play on Rob's insecurities in a way that other lifestyles which differ from his own have not—his attitude to people with different musical tastes, for instance, varies between contempt and total lack of interest. However, he suddenly feels embarrassed about his own lack of a career and about the immaturity of his own life choice, compared to the suited man. While Rob is aware of the perceived childishness of his anti-careerism, it seems that he has always accepted it as part of the composite image of Laddishness that he reveres for its cool, laid-back attitude towards women (forgetting birthdays and never calling). His behavior towards women is inextricably linked to Lad behavior in the rest of his life. Rob is unwilling to put in the effort to separate one element of Lad culture from another. Hornby himself points out in *Fever Pitch* the ease with which people infer a whole, packaged identity from a single attribute such as liking football:

> According to a large number of both men and women, masculinity is a shared set of assumptions and values that you can accept or reject [. . . .] It's easy to forget that we can pick and choose. (p. 80)

Rob is shown to make just this mistake in thinking of himself in terms of polarized stereotypes. It takes the appearance of a New Man who he doesn't regard with contempt, and his growing discomfort with some of Barry's more laddish tendencies, to awaken him to the possibility of forging a personal identity which lies somewhere between being a man who calls and a man who does not.

A further concern of the novel is to portray a distinctly masculine subculture, based on musical obsession. This group is not seen as representative of *all* men, in the way that Rob's attitudes towards women are. Instead, they form a minority group who demonstrate patterns of specifically male consumption, shown in Rob's description of his central customer base:

> I get by because of the people who make a special effort to shop here Saturdays—young men—always young men, with John Lennon specs and leather jackets and armfuls of square carrier bags—and because of the mail order: I advertise in the back of the glossy rock magazines, and get letters from young men, always young men, in Manchester and Glasgow and Ottawa, young men who seem to spend a disproportionate amount of their time looking for deleted Smiths singles and 'ORIGINAL NOT RE-RELEASED' underlined Frank Zappa albums. They're as close to being mad as makes no difference. (p. 38)

While this takes place in the specific context of record buying, it is characterized as a gendered tendency, rather than one linked to consumer preferences or particular leisure interests. In *Fever Pitch*, Hornby states outright that obsessive behavior is a masculine province, and one of the defining differences between the sexes:

> I am not saying that the anally retentive woman does not exist, but she is vastly outnumbered by her masculine equivalent; and while there are women with obsessions, they are usually, I think, obsessive about people, or the focus for their obsession changes quickly. (p. 103)

While the phenomenon of male obsessiveness pre-dates the contemporary masculinity crisis, it is still a product of cultural expectations and socially reinforced structures, and as such is subject to some of the insecurities produced by the mood of 1990s gender relations. In *Fever Pitch*, for instance, Hornby discusses the exclusion of his sister from the father-child bonding experience of his early visits to watch Arsenal, since as a girl growing up in the 1960s it was simply assumed she would have no interest in football. Later in the book, he describes the mixed feelings he experiences in the late 1980s when his then partner develops an interest in football and begins to attend Arsenal matches. Her interest, though never an obsession to rival his, nevertheless seems at a primary level to be unnatural to him, and he confesses to using emotional blackmail to ensure that his attendance takes priority over hers. Feelings of insecurity about a "man's place" being usurped by a woman are made more acute in the relatively progressive climate of the present day. However, the tendency that leads to an "obsessive" interest in pursuits such as football is far less pronounced, in Hornby's view, in women than it has been all along in men. Whether or not you agree with this, football audiences continue to be male-dominated, and in *High Fidelity*, record shops like Rob's remain reliant on the bread-and-butter custom of "young men, always young men."

One of Rob's pervasive traits is the desire to revere abstract femininity as some mystical, elevated state: an ideal that is inevitably shattered by the actions of real women. An example of this can be found in his remarks on women's underwear:

> Women's knickers were a terrible disappointment to me when I embarked on my co-habiting career. I never really recovered from the shock of discovering that women do what we do: they save their best pairs for the nights when they know they are going to sleep with somebody. (p. 45)

The use of "we" indicates Rob's implied audience to be male, and thus sympathetic. The shock he describes is connected with a deep-rooted and traditional idea of women being on a pedestal, having the highest possible standards in underwear as they do in morals. The evidence of the underwear undermines Rob's confidence in women as the nobler sex who are obliged to pity men for being helplessly subject to such bestial desires, desires from which women themselves are mercifully free, or (as Rob would claim) certainly more capable of detachment than men are.

When Rob repeats Johnny's own question, "Are you married?" back to him, Johnny's reply is "You think I'd be in this fucking state if I had a wife?" (p. 53). Rob can say nothing in the face of this assertion by the homeless man, that the presence of a woman can maintain civilized living, and in fact constitutes the line between a "real" life and a miserable shell of existence. For Rob, Dick, and the other men in *High Fidelity*, nurturing is something associated with femininity. The narrative does not contradict this. Rather, it shows women fulfilling this nurturing role and being capable of much more besides, while the male method of showing caring, stereotypically "feminine" behavior is by giving one another the opportunity to demonstrate their strong, silent masculinity. Thus, when Dick asks Rob if he wants to talk about Laura leaving, Rob fulfills this contract by refusing the opportunity: "I tell him there's nothing to say, and for a moment I thought he was going to hug me" (p. 54). Relationships between men seem to be beyond the need for analysis or effort; while achieving a successful relationship with a woman is seen as the ultimate challenge, and in Rob's view, a strenuous ethical test:

> Sometimes it seems as though the only way a man can judge his own niceness, his own *decency*, is by looking at his relationships with women—or rather, with prospective or current sexual partners. It's easy enough to be nice to your mates [. . . .] When it comes to girlfriends, though, it's much trickier to be consistently honourable. One moment you're ticking along, cleaning the toilet bowl and expressing your feelings and doing all the things that a modern chap is supposed to do; the next, you're manipulating and sulking and double-dealing with the best of them. I can't work it out. (pp. 61–2)

Man reverts to his essential nature, that of "manipulating, sulking and double-dealing," when the civilizing veneer of female company begins to wear thin. By now, one could feel that Rob is trying to have his cake and eat it, in that he seems to be claiming that men are victims of both their own essential nature *and* of cultural conditioning. Again, women are represented as a group whose standards form the difficult but worthwhile pinnacle for which to aim; they are the focus of the quasi-spiritual nature of Rob's confused search for happiness and a fulfilled life.

Prolific sexual activity, a characteristic of the masculine man, is inevitably a point of anxiety for Rob. At various points he establishes his reasonable, though not excessive, credentials as a man who has "Been Around": "Over three million men in this country have slept with ten or more women. And do they all look like Richard Gere? [. . . .] We're just blokes, because I, even I, am a member of the exclusive three million club. Ten is not so many if you're unmarried and in your mid-thirties" (p. 96).

A certain level of sexual activity is naturalized as the right of even the average man, and striving to increase that level is similarly natural. Rob believes himself to be following an established path of masculine behavior when he celebrates the fact that Laura's new partner has not yet had sex with her by himself having a one night stand with Marie. However, this competitive, Darwinian world of male sexuality can lead to the acute anxiety brought on by Rob's knowledge, from living in close proximity, of the superior sexual stamina of Laura's new boyfriend Ian:

> I don't know why it matters so much [. . . .] I am tragically unskilled in some very important areas. But sex is different; knowing that a successor is better in bed is impossible to take, and I don't know why. (pp. 65–6)

This marks the re-emergence of Rob's New Man side. His anxiety is now not about quantitative success, measured by notches on the bedpost, but about qualitative prowess in being a admirable lover, able to please women. This is portrayed as an overwhelmingly contemporary dilemma in a passage where Rob contemplates the advanced state of late twentieth-century masculinity:

> I'm happy to be a bloke, I think, but sometimes I'm not happy being a bloke in the late twentieth century. Sometimes I'd rather be my dad. He never had to worry about delivering the goods, because he never knew there were any goods to deliver; he never had to worry about how he ranked on my mother's all-time hot one hundred, because he was first and last on the list [. . . .] (What would he say? [. . . .] Probably something like, "Son, stop whingeing. The good fuck wasn't even *invented* in my day, and no matter how many toilets you clean and vegetarian recipes you have to read, you still have more fun than we were ever allowed." And he'd be right, too.) (p. 102)

Rob experiences a rare moment here of being aware of his privileged status as a late twentieth-century male (and one living a relatively affluent lifestyle, as a property-owning Western city-dweller). Cultural discrimination is exercised far more often in Rob's favor than it is used against him, but his lack of perspective on his own life has blinded him to this, and the climate of a 1990s feminist backlash provides a convenient explanation for the reason things have not gone Rob's way: it can be conveniently blamed on the battle of the sexes, rather than anything more personal or anything broader, which requires him to consider factors beyond gender politics. The fact is that, while masculinity is important, for Rob it eventually becomes less important than humanity and loses its power as an excuse for all the less edifying aspects of life. Rob always knew that Laura's career success, her position in life as a financially independent and intelligent woman, was politically admirable and even deserved, but he still couldn't bring himself to like the situation. The novel closes with Rob having come to terms with Laura's strengths and with her dominance in the relationship. As a result, he can begin to reap the rewards of adopting a more relaxed masculine identity, which does not necessitate either a high-powered career or a high-octane sexual lifestyle.

POP MUSIC—PLEASURE, PAIN AND COMMODITY

The politics of listening

It is extremely difficult to define what can be classed as "popular" music. It might be done in terms of what is readily available in mainstream music shops, which in turn is dependent on what is most frequently consumed. This often leads to the assumption that what is "popular" cannot be "good," and arguments over the extent to which these qualities can overlap. However, this knotty debate is startlingly clear cut to Rob, who does not enlarge on a theory of his musical hierarchy, but is absolutely sure of what music is good—The Clash, Marvin Gaye, and Neil Young—and what is bad—Tina Turner, Phil Collins, and The Eagles, to name but a few. Some inferences about his generic musical preferences can be drawn: punk and soul are good, adult-orientated rock is bad, for example. However, there are a number of aspects that reveal the partialities and prejudices of his system; the qualified presence of black music, the role of female artists, and the almost total absence of contemporary mainstream music.

This absence of contemporary music, or at least that of which most readers will have heard, cannot be attributed to a lack of knowledge on the part of Hornby, who is an enthusiastic devotee of pop music and acts as music critic for the *New Yorker*. Moreover, in Hornby's second novel, *About A Boy*, the rise of Kurt Cobain as a central figure in youth culture and the effect of his suicide on that culture, are explored with sensitivity and perception, empathizing with the teenagers concerned. Readers might well ask, then, why Kurt Cobain, or his 1990s peers, do not feature in *High Fidelity*, and why Rob's taste in music is so retrograde. It seems especially strange when one considers that the early and mid-1990s were an exciting time for home-grown British music, dominated by the movement which came to be known as "Britpop," featuring bands such as Blur, Pulp, and Oasis, who were all trying, in various ways, to capture the authentic sense of British (sub)urban life at the time. They aimed to be contemporary and relevant, bringing a renewed sense of freshness and quality to mainstream music which had been eclipsed by the "manufactured" artists who dominated the charts in the late 1980s. Rather than playing either Britpop or grunge, though, Rob champions artists who are associated with either the punk rock movement of the late 1970s (such as The Clash and Elvis Costello), blue-collar rock as exemplified by Bruce Springsteen, or what could be called black music for white consumption—

for example, soul artists such as Aretha Franklin and Marvin Gaye. The result is that, for such a contemporary novel, its musical content is strangely historical.

The implications of this can be best grasped by considering what Rob does *not* listen to. For example, while he might seem to favor 1970s rock, this doesn't include progressive rock, with its public school and intellectual associations, or glam-rock, which explores areas of gender ambiguity. Rob's hierarchy prioritizes music which remains strictly within gendered boundaries, being either feminized in its expressions of emotion, like soul, or aggressive and anti-intellectual, like punk. In other words, his musical preferences are very much orientated towards a discerning, but nevertheless working-class, white male consumer. Rather than reflecting objective standards of what is best in the culture of pop music, Rob's tastes are grounded in his own youthful experiences and aspirations. As a result, he refuses to update himself or his tastes, since that would mean letting go of the only aspirations he has. In the process, however, he compromises his role as musical guru.

The politics of Rob's musical taste, then, represent a backlash against the need for contemporaneity in music. What he values is timelessness and, in conjunction with this, the nostalgia his musical choices represent. What he rails against can be summarized by his recollection of Ian's musical tastes as: "African, Latin, Bulgarian, whatever fucking world music fad was trendy that week" (p. 64). Rob's antagonism is toward music outside what is either actual, or aspirational, for him. Therefore politicized music, records which are not British or American, or any recently developed musical innovation, are anathema since they would require him to expand his horizons. Fully considering the politics of Rob's musical tastes brings a larger understanding of how insular a character he is, and adds a layer of meaning to the novel. However, one does not need an extensive knowledge of musical genres and the way they are consumed to appreciate Rob's central difficulty with pop music, which lies in the sheer force of its influence on his daily life.

Music as autobiography and aspiration

In spite of Rob's liking for "authenticity," music as realism is not what he seeks: he wants it to be transcendental. Part of the lesson he learns is the need to live with realistic narratives and experiences, rather than over-valuing the transcendental. Authenticity is itself a construct, but Rob's awareness of that does not necessarily control his pursuit of it—he wants to own a "real" record shop, but still a special one: "It's a narrow and dirty and dingy and overcrowded shop, partly because that's what I wanted—this is what record shops should look like" (p. 40). He wants the shop to appeal to more selective customers than the usual record-buying crowd. However, he also wants to distinguish himself from his own customers, the "young men, always young men," for whom visiting Championship Vinyl on Saturdays is their weekly highlight. Rob wants to acquire a stake in the musical lifestyle, in a way which is more special and "authentic" than being a consumer. Running a record shop has not satisfied this desire since it involves selling the same type of product repeatedly, rather than experiencing the supposed originality of the rock star. The nearest he comes to this is in the relationship he fantasizes about having with Marie LaSalle, where she would write songs about him and sing them to an adoring worldwide audience—"This is how I imagined it would be, going out with someone who had a recording contract" (p. 111). The closer he gets to music, or those who make it, the more he feels alive and special.

Rob's view of the pop music's emotional power locates it in the same sphere occupied by the novel, as a new and subversive art form, in the nineteenth century; a sphere which has since been occupied by films, TV, various new musical forms, and most recently the Internet. His position is slightly different from the hostility of mid-twentieth century cultural critics to the corrupting powers of rock 'n' roll, focusing more on the empathy he feels with young people's emotional extremes:

> People worry about kids playing with guns, and teenagers watching violent videos: we are scared that some sort of culture of violence will take them over. Nobody worries about kids listening to thousands—literally thousands—of songs about broken hearts and rejection and pain and misery and loss. (p. 27)

Pop music's insidiousness, it seems, is the source of its danger. It has come to be regarded as part of the cultural furniture. Rob demonstrates its power to engage us, even if he overtly warns us against emulating this to his own obsessive degree. Here Rob manages to be both helpless consumer and concerned critic, analyzing and enjoying the culture in which he lives in a satisfyingly postmodern way. He considers himself an authority on music, while also being deeply embedded into it, so much so that he cannot extricate his own life from the music he listens to and vice versa. He enhances his dented sense of self-esteem after Laura's departure by rearranging his records into "autobiographical" order: "What I really like is the feeling of security I get from my new filing system; I have made myself more complicated than I really am. I have a couple of thousand records, and you have to be me—or, at the very least, a doctor of Flemingology—to know how to find any of them" (p. 52).

In defining himself as the sum of his record collection, Rob now feels that he is more than the sum of its parts. As a result, he is caught between the conviction that music and life are interchangeable—since for him, they are—and the awareness that, for most people, pop music is merely a leisure activity, a consumer habit—something which permits an escape from themselves and their lives.

What Rob does not want to do is compartmentalize his love of music as something which is just one facet of his character. As with his approach to masculinity, he feels that he has committed himself to a package in which his life and his love of music are inseparable. Rather than being a discriminating consumer, he wants to be utterly consumed: "I'd like my life to be like a Bruce Springsteen song [. . . .] I know that I'm not born to run, I know that the Seven Sisters Road is nothing like Thunder Road, but *feelings* can't be so different, can they?" (p. 130).

Rob's imperviousness to the emotional complexities of his relationships with women (or people in general) exists alongside his eagerness to participate in the feelings generated by a song. This is exactly the danger that Rob himself pointed out, which is that the emotional rewards offered by a pop song can rival and even outdo real life, by being more compelling and easier to assimilate than the messiness of emotions excited by people. By purchasing complexity in the form of more and more records, he can avoid having to develop complexity himself; he prefers being a consumer to being a creator, because involvement with cultural artefacts like records can be prolonged indefinitely, played again and again. Trying to apply the same techniques to life results in the absence of relationships, which are stuck, as it were, on repeat:

> If you place music (and books, probably, and films, and plays, and anything that makes you *feel*) at the centre of your being, then you can't afford to sort out your love life, start to think of it as the finished product. You've got to pick at it, keep it alive and in turmoil. (p. 138)

As with masculinity, however, music doesn't have to be discarded wholesale, but rather redefined in a new, relative system of values where it can exist alongside real-life relationships, in a mode of life where Rob's previous hierarchical structures are dismantled. This de-centering of his obsession in favor of a more fluid, varied range of aspirations in life which can accommodate the importance of both Laura and The Clash suggest that as well as the *bildungsroman* model, the effects of postmodernism can be seen in the new world order of *High Fidelity*.

POSTMODERNITY

Postmodernism is perhaps even more difficult to define than popular music. Furthermore, it is less obviously relevant to *High Fidelity*. However, since the novel's concern with the contemporary is so important, and since postmodernism is considered to be a defining condition of contemporary life and a great deal of contemporary literature, it seems worthwhile to examine the relationship between *High Fidelity* and the postmodern.

Postmodernism is a complex phenomenon, but can be described in terms of a few broad characteristics for my purposes here. Some of these provide continuity with its predecessor, modernism, while others break from it. Briefly, modernist and postmodernist works share:

- Self-consciousness and reflexivity; being aware of themselves as texts
- Fragmented or multiple views of life experience
- Skepticism about the autonomy of the human subject or individual

Modernist works (for example, T. S. Eliot's poem *The Waste Land*) are often pessimistic about these aspects of modern life, turning to art as a means of redemption. In contrast, postmodernists tend to be celebratory about these developments, seeing their art as embedded in modern culture. Some of the distinctive qualities of postmodernism are:

- Promoting the breakdown between "high" and "low" culture
- Critiquing "grand narratives" or "metanarratives": systems that explain and order how the world works, such as capitalism, religion, or democracy
- Constructing "virtual" and alternative realities which compete with and supersede actual reality—for example, media images, copies of artworks which become widely available, or "tribute" rock groups
- The use of irony, parody, and pastiche to create texts, moving away from any ideal of "originality," which is now seen as impossible

Postmodernism began as an *enfant terrible* aiming to shake up established cultural values and views and has been successful enough to be regarded now as part of the literary establishment. Put simply, postmodernism is almost expected to be in the repertoire of a literary novelist. Indeed, its presence is often regarded as a quality which separates the literary from the popular; for a movement which seeks to erode the difference between high and low culture, postmodernism itself is generally a high-brow interest, discussed mostly by the educated elite. This has led to accusations of insularity, with postmodern theory being categorized as self-justifying and self-perpetuating—irrelevant to the everyday lives of the majority. Dominic Strinati, for example, states that:

> The debate seems to have been much more involved with the theory of postmodernism than with its recognition as an empirical phenomenon.

Relatively few writers appear to have asked the question: can we see postmodernism in the world around us? (Strinati, 223)

Nick Hornby, I believe, is one of the few writers who have done so. Since *High Fidelity* is first and foremost a popular novel—though for many critics it crosses into literary territory—and a novel primarily concerned with the events of everyday lives, postmodernism would seem to be an irrelevance to the world it describes. However, this would be inaccurate. While postmodernism may not be a subject of consideration to most of us on a daily basis, its theorists would argue that we cannot help, living in the historical period that we do, being postmodern subjects—we live, whether we like it or not, in the "postmodern condition." Rob is an example of how one can experience in many ways the feeling of being a helplessly postmodern subject, who, as a consequence of certain historical and cultural developments, lives with the fact that certain barriers have broken down and that fixed ideas about truth, justice, art, and progress are impossible to sustain. On the other hand, certain central tenets of postmodernism, such as the debunking of "grand narratives" and the apparent breakdown of a distinction between art and popular culture, are themselves shown to be extremely difficult to sustain by the events of *High Fidelity*. This section will examine some of the postmodern and anti-postmodern aspects of the novel in order to assess the relation between Hornby's text and the literary cult of the postmodern.

Our postmodern world is, supposedly, one in which reality is defined and constructed by the media and by media images, rather than vice versa. Personal identity is no longer something fixed and reliable, but flexible and constructed by a variety of images and "virtual realities." Rob's experiences can be seen to conform in many ways to this view of the world; his reality is constructed largely through the consumption of pop music, as is his idea of who he is and what his life means—if it means anything at all. However, the misery of much of Rob's narrative contrasts with the positive, celebratory tone of that which is intentionally postmodern. Unlike postmodern theorists, he seems less than happy about this state of affairs and is frequently dogged by guilt, pain, and embarrassment about the conditions of his life. Moreover, he seems ultimately to reject the "play" of different images and modes of existence for a conventional, humanistic "grand narrative," involving the choice of monogamy, a settled occupation, and the ideals of personal development and maturity we have already seen as part of a *bildungsroman* pattern.

Rob's lifelong obsession with pop music could in itself be regarded as a "grand narrative," which has governed his life and given it meaning. In that case, there are two ways to read the ending of the novel. First, it could be seen as enacting the exchange of one grand narrative (music) for another (romantic partnership). Alternatively, though, it could be seen as allowing a new system in which neither music nor romantic relationships need to be part of a hierarchy, where one or the other is the "center" of Rob's life, but where both can be enjoyed without being mutually exclusive. This does not invalidate the earlier view of the novel as a *bildungsroman* narrative; it puts Rob's accomplishment of personal growth into the context where, as a more mature and complex person, he can have both a more stable lifestyle and a more fluid one, having abandoned the rigid ideas about personal relationships and cultural values that held him immobile. That balanced lifestyle demands, if it is to work, a belief in concepts like social responsibility, self-identity, and a "center" to the world, concepts which under the governance of postmodernism have been deemed mistaken.

In many ways a useful definition of postmodernism, especially in relation to *High Fidelity*, is that it functions as an antithesis to the qualities of *bildungsroman* that I discussed earlier. Where *bildungs-*

roman pursues an ethical code and spiritual meaning, postmodernism is gleefully materialistic, dwelling resolutely in a world of images, brand names, and virtual existence. *Bildungsroman* is based on a linear model of development and progress (for both the individual and the community), a concept that postmodernism deconstructs in favor of a circular, de-centered view of history, personal identity, and life in general. Rob aspires to perform this kind of deconstruction on himself and his own identity by constructing the "history" of his choice when he moves to London: "I was old enough to have a history. At home I didn't have a history, just stuff that everybody already knew, and that therefore wasn't worth repeating" (p. 25).

The word "history" might seem to evoke realism and authenticity. Here, though, it signifies a very different construct: the freedom Rob has to fabricate a history for himself which, ironically, he does for the effect of making himself seem more authentic, complex, and interesting—the faked Rob becomes, in fact, the "real" one. The way that this confusion passes almost unnoticed, as an unremarkable part of the narrative, shows the extent to which we regard "reality" as a negotiable quality, not necessarily to be based in historical facts which are themselves a doubtful concept. This rearrangement of knowledge as "history," and "stuff that everyone already knew," balances the values of *bildungsroman* and those of postmodernism which will be maintained throughout the novel.

Being serious: gender and culture

The most frequently name-checked commodity in *High Fidelity* is music. References to fiction form a low-key but still significant presence. Rob's self-definition includes a statement about his attitude to so-called "literature": "I've read books like *The Unbearable Lightness of Being* (they were about girls, right?)" (p. 29). This tells us a lot about the self-image Rob chooses to project: he wishes to be seen as someone who is cultured to an extent which is fashionable in contemporary society (which does not necessitate claims to have read Dickens or James Joyce, or anything pre-1960s) but who chooses to wear their cultural knowledge lightly, and certainly not to take the "serious" literature they have read too seriously. Seriousness, in fact (as opposed to the fanaticism exhibited by Rob and his co-workers) is to be mocked whenever possible. This does not mean, however, that Rob ignores or dislikes such cultural markers being displayed by women. On the contrary, his survey of the flat after Laura's departure name-checks her "half-read Julian Barnes paperback" (p. 45). And while at Marie's, waiting with studied casualness for their night of passion to begin, he occupies himself by "browsing through her John Irving paperback" (p. 107).

Women, it seems, have greater dispensation to indulge in cultural activities, and Rob expects them to be more interested in higher levels of culture than himself. He prefers his sexual partners to demonstrate a certain level of knowledge, and takes some pride in not sleeping with the culturally ignorant. His earlier obsession with Charlie demonstrates his need to find a partner who possesses cultural and social charisma and also his fear that too high a regard for these qualities is unattractive and needs to be suppressed. Rob exemplifies a view of women as being innately more comfortable with high culture and "seriousness": the very things he, as a man, wishes to admire but also to avoid.

Repetitions

Rob's mother represents an earlier generation who are dismayed by the impermanence of things they took for granted, such as courtship and its inevitable consequence, marriage. In reply to Rob's "That's not what happens now," she says: "I don't know what does happen now. Apart from you meet someone, you move in together, she goes. You meet someone, you move in together, she goes" (p. 49).

It is not so much the decay of the institution of marriage but the fragility of life patterns that is the source of dismay here. While at first this temporality is one of Rob's comforts in life, the novel ends with him becoming dissatisfied with his own fear of stability, to the point where he actually proposes marriage to Laura. Her refusal allows the novel to avoid the clichéd happy ending of romance and to end poised between the polarities of *bildungsroman* and postmodernity, growing up and repetition, that it has maintained throughout. Rob gets to grow up by repeating the highlight of his career as a DJ; similarly, his relationship with Laura moves onto a new level of stability without conforming to the traditional requirement of marriage.

Rob is not the sole beneficiary of his partnership with Laura, although it may often seem that way. He remarks on his ability to make her laugh, observing that: "She complains frequently about my 'relentless triviality' but it has its uses" (p. 78). Rob provides an escape for Laura from excessive realism, from the grim hardships that she has to confront as a lawyer. Laura's wish for some real depth in her life finds some welcome relief in Rob's determination to stay on the surface; her "intensity" can be reduced to a bearable level. The beneficial effects of postmodernism, then, are felt more keenly in regular and regulated doses than as a fully endorsed lifestyle. Rob's description of the feelings of a compulsive Saturday afternoon record-buyer exemplifies this:

> You walk much more quickly afterwards, trying to recapture the part of the day that has escaped, and quite often you have the urge to read the international section of a newspaper, or go to see a Peter Greenaway film, to consume something solid and meaty which will lie on top of the candy-floss worthlessness clogging up your head. (p. 82)

This feeling that there is something more substantial that should *also* be consumed, that an ephemeral cultural experience should be counterbalanced by something "solid and meaty" is one which seems to constitute a spirited rebellion against the superficiality of postmodern life. However, there are a number of factors which disrupt this rebellion. First, there is the sheer pleasure of postmodern consumption, which has led Rob to spend most of his life fighting the need for depth. Second, there is the fact that Rob, without any conscious motivation, has always exercised the characteristically postmodern judgement in which political events are deemed equivalent to a good chord change: an example is provided by one of his remarks early in the conversation between himself and Laura, as they drive to visit her newly bereaved mother near the end of the novel. He asks her in horror: "How can you like Art Garfunkel *and* Solomon Burke? It's like saying you supporting the Israelis *and* the Palestinians" (p. 208).

As this conversation brings out many of the contradictions and confusions involved in cultural judgements and postmodernity, I am going to examine it in detail in order to demonstrate how complex the novel's treatment of the postmodern condition is.

McDonalds v. Burger King—the abdication of judgement

Laura retaliates to this challenge by defending her preference for Art Garfunkel's "Bright Eyes" as follows:

> I can see why you prefer Solomon to Art. I understand, really I do. And if I was asked to say which of the two was better, I'd go for Solomon every time. He's authentic, and black, and legendary, and all that sort of thing. But I like "Bright Eyes." I think it's got a pretty tune, and beyond that, I don't really care. There are so many other things to worry about. I know I

> sound like your mum, but they're only pop records, and if one's better than another, who cares, really, apart from you and Barry and Dick? To me, it's like arguing the difference between McDonalds and Burger King. I'm sure there must be one, but who can be bothered to find out what it is? (p. 209)

In stating that she prefers the non-authentic tune, for superficial aesthetic reasons, Laura manages to occupy both a modernist position (classifying artefacts of low culture is not really important in the Grand Scheme of Life) and a postmodernist one, in which judging one cultural artefact to be better than another is irrelevant and therefore invalid, since if no one can be bothered to determine the difference between McDonalds and Burger King, then for all practical purposes, there is not one. The group to whom such things matter (people like Rob, who has "complicated and informed views on the subject") are a minority who can be discounted. They are elitists, vainly resisting the democratization of culture which equates Solomon Burke with Art Garfunkel.

Laura also shows a retained deference to modernist and realist ideals, revealed in her guilt about recognizing Solomon's artistic superiority. "Authentic" is employed as a term of praise, while its inclusion in a string of descriptive adjectives without a referent (what is Burke an "authentic" example of, exactly? It does not seem to matter) reduce it to another construct, without any defined basis in the reality of Burke's existence and musical career. The fact that "it doesn't really matter—they're only pop records"—suggests the continuance of a grand narrative in which political events take precedence over consumer preferences. If that is the case, then why has a whole narrative been constructed around the path to personal development which has emerged out of an interest in a "trivial" cultural interest like pop music? It could be argued that for Rob, pop music has truly been a grand narrative, one which he debunks by dethroning it from its central place in his life, reducing it to merely one of a number of competing narratives, and thus scoring a victory for postmodernism. Alternatively, he could be seen (as I argued earlier) as finally being reclaimed for the path of humanism, returning to the grand narrative of personal development and maturity from which he strayed in his youth.

The significant factor in making these interpretations is one of choice. Laura's assessment of the relative merits of Burke and Garfunkel is very much an *unwitting* endorsement of postmodernism, rather than a conscious decision to extend this form of anti-judgement to life as a whole. Similarly, Rob sees the attractive consequences of living in a postmodern world, such as being able to construct himself anew, and being able to avoid permanency, but ultimately tires of them and feels guilty about his lack of "substance" and the absence of a grand narrative for his life.

Dominic Strinati has pointed out the paradox that postmodernism, in seeking to explain the inadequacy of grand narratives, takes on itself the characteristics and claimed authority of just such a grand narrative. *High Fidelity* demonstrates this: Rob accepts certain postmodern aspects of life as enjoyable and appealing, but refuses to embrace it as a way of life. He craves a grand narrative that makes more conventional sense, that involves certain abiding standards, and that has a center. What he also craves, however, is the option to deviate from that narrative and consume something new, while knowing that this risks disrupting the rewards of having a center for his life: "What's wrong with Laura is that I'll never see her for the first or second or third time again" (p. 247).

Rob realizes that, like his customers, he needs repeatedly to procure what is familiar (the romantic experience of meeting a woman) through consuming more and more examples of the same product, whether records or girlfriends. This is the aspect of Rob which is most postmodern—his acknowledged desire to repeat, pastiche, and mindlessly consume experiences without feeling the need to move them onto a "deeper" level. The superficial level on which he operates is what he imagines to be the most gratifying one, avoiding the need to engage with life changing experiences like partnership or death, and embracing the infinite play and apparent renewal promised by the particular sphere of music-related consumerism that is Rob's chosen lifestyle. Without being a postmodern novel, *High Fidelity* nevertheless takes on the challenge of depicting what could be called "applied postmodernism": presenting a fictional examination of its "real life" effects in the way that Strinati cites as lacking in most discussions of the topic. Hornby's "realistic" take on postmodernism manages to be accommodating towards material pleasures, while still affirming human values of love and personal relationships as giving late twentieth-century life its meaning.

Hornby is not afraid to tackle old-fashioned themes relating to the meaning of life; how a person can live a good life, and what kind of moral framework should guide one's behavior towards others. He does this, though, without being an old-fashioned writer. He uses literature for the kind of purpose it has traditionally been held to have: to interrogate the values of the world in which it has been constructed. In a postmodern world, those values are intent on deconstructing the worth of that sort of interrogation, in favor of a playful exploration of relative and shifting values. In his most recent novel, *How To Be Good*, Hornby has become more ambitious and is more explicit about the seriousness of his purposes and his subject matter. The title is self-explanatory, even though the novel itself does not come up with anything so glib as the answer to that question. To say that *High Fidelity* has more lightness of touch might make the later novel sound unwieldy, which it is not. However, this lightness of touch manifests itself in the ease and subtlety with which it accomplishes both its overt purpose—to be comedic and entertaining—while maintaining its underlying seriousness of theme and largeness of scope.

The Novel's Reception

On its publication in 1995, *High Fidelity* enjoyed an unusual status as a first novel which came from a familiar point of view, written by an author with previous form. It was eagerly awaited as the first work of fiction from a writer who was already well known because of *Fever Pitch*: a book difficult to categorize but appreciated for its originality and freshness. There was a sense that these qualities would make for an interesting fictional debut on Hornby's part. At the same time, however, Hornby was an unproven first-time novelist, with reviewers waiting to see whether his writing abilities would transfer well to the fictional arena. In short, this was Hornby's opportunity to prove himself more than a one-hit wonder in a specialized field, and to demonstrate the broader applicability of his talents.

On the whole, *High Fidelity* was reviewed extremely positively, gaining admiration from both British and American critics and acclaim from its large number of readers. The online book-sellers, Amazon.com, provide a facility on their website for readers to contribute reviews of novels they have read and purchased, and this resource offers a fascinating insight into the perspective of the "ordinary reader" on Hornby's work. However, a novel's critical reputation is still formed mainly on the basis of judgements made by a small number of professional reviewers in newspapers and periodicals. It is worth examining what common conclusions are drawn about *High Fidelity* in this context, and on what points, if any, reviewers disagree about the novel's merits.

REALISM AND "BEING REALISTIC"

Suzanne Moore's review of *High Fidelity* in *The Guardian* began with the statement, "I have known quite a few men like Rob Fleming, the central character of Nick Hornby's first novel," a sentiment which is repeated in countless other reviews. The accuracy of Hornby's portrayal of a certain type of male adult is admired repeatedly: Rob is a character who is primarily familiar not as a type of fictional protagonist, but as the likeness of someone known, in real life, to the reader. This is not to say, of course, that he can not resemble both, as Rob Nixon pointed out in his review of the novel in the *New Yorker*: "As a creation, Rob is a completely realized individual, but there are lots of guys like him around—underqualified guys, dead-ended in their jobs, attached to women who are smarter, have credentials, and are on the move."

Nixon implied that "completely realized" literary creations will somehow be different from the kind of person you might actually meet. This kind of surprise that literature and life might resemble one another can be attributed to the literary mores of the late twentieth century which favor irony, distance, and sophisticated postmodern sensibilities. Hornby's reviewers seem startled, but pleasantly so, at finding a protagonist who reminds them of people they know. This apparent rebound from current literary fashion, though, can lead to approval on those grounds just as it can invite criticism, as Nixon demonstrated later in his review: "In writing about this very contemporary type, Hornby refuses the false choice between male backlash and fiction that is bloodlessly P.C. *High Fidelity* stakes out a territory both more complex and more nearly true to life."

The contemporaneity of Hornby's work, another feature for which it is frequently commended, can be seen to condemn or to exalt the culture of 1990s men that Rob Fleming represents. Nixon approved of Hornby's decision to portray a middle ground that is "more complex and more true to life." The separation of these two terms demonstrates the way in which complexity is more often associated with literariness (which in turn is often linked with difficulty and elaborateness of style) than it is with being realistic. Though Hornby's novel is clearly a work of "realist" fiction, these responses show very clearly that realism and "realistic" fiction are two different things, both likely to be regarded as somewhat anachronistic. With regard to *High Fidelity*, the consensus seems to be that Hornby has redeemed his old-fashioned approach by the obvious relevance and applicability of his narrative to contemporary life, so much so that his work is "realist" in its broad appeal. Suzanne Moore stated that: "He has a purchase on 'the universal.' Hornby's purchase feels so effortless that his is a pop book in the best sense of the word."

Michelle Huneven's review of the novel for the *Los Angeles Times* was unusual in its relatively ungendered view of Rob's trials; unlike many other reviews, no comment is offered about the masculinity of Rob's particular character traits. It is difficult to tell whether she rose above this view of the novel or simply overlooked it: since she called the book "Hornby's second novel," there is evidence to suggest some oversights in her analysis. However, like Moore, she applied the term "universal" to describe the portrayal of Rob's experiences: "The transition he faces at 35, newly single, deep in a rut, is a near-universal one: sooner or later, the fiercely held truths embraced early on in life fail to carry you past a certain point." Part of Hornby's realism is, as I argued in the previous section, connected with *High Fidelity*'s status as *bildungsroman*, a novel of development, and Huneven, like other reviewers, drew attention to the importance of Rob's reluctant quest for maturity. They rightly focused on the importance of character development in *High Fidelity*, and of the novel's portrayal of this as a stuttering, stop-start process that can only happen when Rob actually realizes that he *is* immature and *wants* to be different. David Horspool, in the *Times Literary Supplement*, pointed out the corresponding sin of creating an endlessly philosophizing narrator as one that Hornby has avoided: "[Rob's search for 'something else':] It is an admission that, for all its importance, soul-searching can be destructive if it never leads anywhere [. . . .] It is, for Rob, a constant, but constantly stifled process."

Hornby gained approval for the fact that Rob's transition to adulthood is neither smooth nor perfectly realized, and that he can change without having to be rendered, in the *denouement*, as a fully rehabilitated, well-balanced specimen of manhood. Both Rob and the process of his development remain appealingly imperfect, while being satisfying enough for the majority of reviewers.

There was enthusiasm from reviewers of the novel for the ideas of gender differences and gendered foibles that *High Fidelity* describes. Some of the traits ascribed specifically to men, though, are also celebrated as being part of the novel's "universalism"—namely, the emotional power of music, and especially pop music, to affect our everyday lives and feelings. John Harvey declared the value of this in the *San Francisco Chronicle*: "Hornby is excellent at delineating the importance of popular music in the lives of Rob and his friends—and, by implication, all of our lives." This statement is quite challenging, as many other reviewers were at pains to point out that they knew people like Rob, Dick, and Barry, without resembling them in any way themselves. But Harvey's point was that while this brand of musical snobbery may belong to a certain type of person, a far more common experience is the mixed feeling of nostalgia and anticipation, as Rob describes it, that pop music evokes. The importance of this effect, whether it is welcomed or not, has to be recognized.

Mick Brown, in the *Independent*, observed that for Rob: "Constant exposure to the emotional textbook of popular music has resulted in emotional retardation." However, this constant exposure is something that is common to huge numbers of people in the contemporary world. As such, while Hornby may be writing about a male reaction, he is nevertheless writing about a universal experience, and one whose potency has, according to *High Fidelity*, yet to be fully understood.

MEN'S STUFF

High Fidelity was immediately seen as a defining text for the late-twentieth century male, and also as a novel which established a new genre of male relationship fiction. Many reviewers observed the link between *Fever Pitch* and *High Fidelity* and identified Hornby as a talented chronicler of male obsessions. Nixon in the *New Yorker* wrote that, "In the space of two books, Hornby has established himself as a maestro of the male confessional." The "confessional" mode that Hornby employs in *High Fidelity*, however, was in some instances viewed as going beyond narrative technique and signifying autobiographical input, perhaps because of the obvious personal investment in *Fever Pitch*. Horspool explicitly linked this aspect of the two books: "The book [*Fever Pitch*] seemed to be a form oftherapy for the author. *High Fidelity*, Hornby's first novel, gives the same impression."

Projecting the events of the novel on to Hornby seems to take a rather limited view of him as a writer, implying that *High Fidelity* is a second volume of autobiography, thinly disguised. This ignores the conscious use of novelistic technique in *High Fidelity*, and the fact that *Fever Pitch* is more of a novelistic autobiography, in its presentation of events and its "plot" of eventual footballing success, than *High Fidelity* is an autobiographical novel. Nixon's term, "confessional," seems much more appropriate; further on in his review, he also highlighted the irony of the term: "Men in Hornby's world are often trying to say things to each other in ways that prevent anything from getting said." This comment picked up on the fact that *High Fidelity* portrays men having difficulties in communicating with each other as well as with women, though their problems with the latter get more attention. Astute reviewers also picked up on the deliberate speciousness of Rob's reasoning that men are unavoidably conditioned to behave in this way and that nothing can be done about it. Horspool recognized, in his *Times Literary Supplement* review, Hornby's sophistication in creating a narrator who is at turns both obtuse and crafty, noting that: "Rob's emotional maturity is not matched by an intellectual one." The argument that men simply are not capable, which Rob falls back on more than once, is defeated by Catch-22-style logic. Articulating his argument so persuasively shows that he has the intellectual capacity to see the self-justifying nature of his chosen approach to relationships, but that he lacks the desire to change it.

In spite of its universal qualities, *High Fidelity* was also received as a novel about specifically contemporary issues, and perhaps the most prominent of those was the "crisis in masculinity." Suzanne Moore, again, discerned that this is an issue relevant both to a particular minority, and also to a wider group, when she used the phrase "mid-life crisis" in relation to Rob:

> I hesitate to use such an unspecific term. Applied to men, "mid-life crisis" does not describe a passing phase, but the state of mind of any male over 30. In many ways, this is a coming-of-age novel for those who have spent their entire lives avoiding the issue for fear of coming too soon.

Moore highlighted the *bildungsroman* theme of self-development, and noted that fictional men of Rob's generation are now running away from the maturity process rather than embracing it—as female protagonists, who have had to fight for entry to the genre, might be more likely to do. Hornby is perceived by reviewers in general to be treading a thin line between explaining and excusing the worst behaviors of men like Rob. His ultimate success is based on the novel's integration of realist and comic properties which itself is achieved, according to Moore, by Hornby's skill as a novelist: "In lesser hands, this tale could have become another psychobabble book about men's 'inability to commit', or 'fear of intimacy'. But Hornby is such a terrific writer that *High Fidelity* is totally charming as well as being laugh-out-loud funny."

The reference to "psychobabble" makes the same point as Nixon's reference to "P.C.": identifying Hornby as a writer opposed to these theories and fashions, opposed to drawing on the discourse of either self-help or equal opportunities. This is not, perhaps, entirely accurate—many ordinary readers do indeed see *High Fidelity* as something of a self-help text. Indeed, using it in this way is endorsed on the original paperback edition of the novel itself, which quotes Harry Enfield, writing in the *Independent on Sunday*, as saying, "If you are male, you should read it and then make your partner read it, so that they will no longer hate you but pity you instead."

However, while Rob initially scorns the jargon and superficial values of political correctness and equal rights, he ends up being won over to the kind of liberal values that political correctness is supposed to champion. It can be argued that Hornby ends up having his cake and eating it: he gets away with espousing inclusive values while he also receives the kudos awarded to those who make fun of a politically inclusive vocabulary.

As *High Fidelity* is portrayed so strongly as a book about men, it may be unsurprising that little comment is made about the novel's female characters. Mick Brown in the *Independent* was an exception to this, commending the accuracy of Hornby's leading female protagonist: "In Laura, he has fashioned a wonderfully knowing and sympathetic portrait of a woman with a mind of her own, but a woman capable of saving Rob from himself." It is good to see this recognized, since *High Fidelity* has a range of well-crafted female characters, from Liz the friend and "paranoid feminist," to Rob's fretting mother.

AUDIO STYLE

In keeping with the image of *High Fidelity* as "confessional," many reviewers commented on the appropriately vocal qualities of the novel. Michelle Huneven stated: "*High Fidelity*, like any good pop song, is a voice piece: confessional, deceptively simple, haunting and, well, a bit pat." The first-person narration is particularly effective in creating this sense of a spoken conversation or confession. Rob Nixon, similarly, stated: "Hornby has got Rob's chatty mania, his involuted record-driven riffs, down pat: appropriately for a music novel, *High Fidelity* is writing for the ear." Nixon's approval of Hornby's work as an integration of style and content was stronger than Huneven's where the comparison to a pop song is largely, but not entirely, flattering. Suzanne Moore's comparison is straightforwardly positive: "Reading *High Fidelity* is like listening to a great single [. . .] an instant classic."

I wonder whether this analogy is as favorable as it seems. Is being an "instant classic" different from being a long-term success? Other reviews, in places, suggest that Hornby is still mining the seam from which *Fever Pitch* came, and these reviewers reserve judgement on his overall capabilities as an author. Charles Hopkinson's review in the *Independent On Sunday* commented on the vocal similarities between the two books: "So close is the tone to that of *Fever Pitch* that the reader's instinct is to accept the intimacy of the voice, allowing it to obliterate the distinction between fact and fiction." Hopkinson left open the question of whether he thought this offered a laudable challenge or a potential minefield to the reader. On the other hand, John Harvey again employed a musical analogy in order to extend a positive judgement: "This is an enjoyable and eminently readable book, fresh as 'Revolver', say, or 'Rubber Soul', when those Beatles albums were new in the charts." This comparison elevated *High Fidelity* further, as both a fresh new "sound," and also a text that was likely to become a popular classic in the manner of those Beatles albums.

BRITISH OR UNIVERSAL?

In spite of commenting widely on the universal qualities of *High Fidelity*, reviewers seemed split on the implications of the way that national cultures are portrayed in the novel. Personal loyalties and perspectives creep in here to some extent—Suzanne Moore's hitherto fair-minded review took a surprising turn near the end by remarking that: "Hornby, thankfully, doesn't want to be American or aimlessly clever."

This observation perhaps overlooked the sincere veneration in the novel for the richness of American musical culture. Rob's musical ideals are divided between American or American-influenced rock and soul, and British punk-era, which hardly allows for a dismissal of all things American. Indeed, Hornby himself has repeatedly talked about his admiration for American writers and his own strong preference for contemporary American literature over British. Nevertheless, the novel's portrayal of a distinctly British culture—which is an aspect of the novel separate from its universalism—is also important, and was remarked upon by Michelle Huneven: "In America, we call making a life commitment to a person or a job 'settling down.' The British call it 'sorting things out,' a phrase that adds a sense of parity and removes some of the implied disappointment from the transaction."

"Settling down" is actually also used in Britain, probably as often as "sorting things out," but Huneven's awareness of the Britishness—and therefore possible strangeness—of some aspects of the novel is welcome. John Harvey, again, actively celebrated the differences than American readers would find: "The other thing that this novel presents superbly to American readers is the peculiarly English male psyche, one that excels at self-admonition and failure and will make only rare and usually doomed forays upon success."

LIMITATIONS

For all its praiseworthy qualities, faults can be found—and were—in *High Fidelity*. Most of the critical elements of reviews centered on either the scope of the novel or the manner of its resolution as being untrue to the misery and black humor that had largely preceded it. Suzanne Moore both acknowledged and defended Hornby from the former charge: "Only the especially crabby could complain that Hornby is not writing about the state of the nation, the underclass, the overclass, weird sex or bad drugs or living on the edge. *High Fidelity* is about people, men and women in the middle, in a muddle."

To be fair, this "crabby" view was almost entirely absent from the novel's reception. It seems to have been accepted that Hornby was writing about a particular and familiar social milieu, and had chosen his fictional ground carefully on that basis. The second criticism, that the novel's ending is too saccharine to be true to the complexities raised earlier in the narrative, is harder to dismiss. Michelle Huneven stated that Hornby tries too hard to be ultimately comprehensive: "Sometimes, especially towards the end of the book, it feels as if the author himself is a little too systematic, as if every one of Rob's issues—from instant infatuations to forcing compilation tapes on his girlfriends—needs to be addressed."

Rob Nixon focused his doubts on the apparent smoothing of Rob's path to redemption, which he sees as a sudden swerve in the direction of the narrative: "For most of *High Fidelity* Rob is grooved on nostalgia; his fingers itch for replay the way smokers itch for cigarettes [. . . .] Perhaps Rob's transformation comes a little fast. Let's just say that the novel's ending is upbeat and romantic—and cunningly movie minded." It can not be denied that the ending is "upbeat and romantic," but it is not entirely unrealistic. Consideration should also be given to the popular fiction market in which *High Fidelity* is intended to compete. It is a comic novel as well as being a slice of social realism, and this element of the novel's composition can be seen to drive its ending.

Huneven was skeptical about the apparent betrayal of some of the novel's asserted values: "The ending is like the last chorus of 'The Last Waltz': everybody on stage, joining in. The question is, can we readers—ourselves the cynical melancholic victims of pop music's imposed misery—suffer such an orchestrated, upbeat, feel-good finale?"

This perception of the contradictions inherent in a critical appreciation of pop music and pop culture is sharp: *High Fidelity* does seem to say that for some people, music is inherently linked with misery. However, that is not to say that they always want it to be that way—the novel shows Rob, eventually, growing out of that cynicism and melancholy, because he has decided that he wants to. Similarly, world-weary readers, well-versed in the conventions of pop music, might indeed decide that they prefer the cynical outlook; they might also decide that they prefer the opportunity of escape from this melancholy. The popularity of the novel suggests that, critical sensibilities apart, the second view prevails among its readers.

As ever, there were also critics who felt this ending to be wholly justified by what has gone before it, and by the general tone of the novel, as Charles Hopkinson did: "If he [Hornby] were less of a romantic, the ending would be different, and perhaps more bracing. But Hornby has earned the right to give Rob a glimpse of heaven: and, unlike *Fever Pitch*, this is not supposed to be real life." This comment brings us back to the fine distinction that exists (however many Rob Flemings one is personally acquainted with) between the fictional realism Hornby has created, and the "real life" he is portraying, rather than documenting as fact. Fictional licence, or "romance" is a permissible and even rightful part of such realism. David Horspool concluded his *Times Literary Supplement* review by endorsing this resolution as a worthy example of traditional literary practice:

> Hornby also shows how contentment with his job and contentment with his girlfriend have to be integrated. [. . . .] He [Rob] may achieve this

realization by compiling a tape of songs that Laura might like, rather than one which he thinks she should like, but Nick Hornby makes it as convincing an epiphany as any.

Horspool's references to "integration" and "realization" being achieved present a view of the novel in which its ending is consonant with expectations, rather than out of step with them. Overall, reviews of the novel endorse this general approval of *High Fidelity*. Its component parts receive differing levels of praise but most reviewers regarded it as a work in which the whole was agreeably greater than the sum of its parts.

4

The Novel's Performance

Since the success of *High Fidelity*, successive works by Hornby have attracted much more attention from reviewers and from the media in general. Although *Fever Pitch* had itself been a groundbreaking success, *High Fidelity* proved Hornby's credentials as a writer of mainstream fiction and paved the way for his graduation to respectful mentions in the *New York Review of Books* and similar publications. *How To Be Good*, his latest novel, has been widely reviewed and was discussed as a serious contender for the UK's Booker Prize shortlist. In the end, the novel was not included but the fact that this decision has since been disparaged shows the increasing claim which Hornby's work has to be part of the literary establishment. *High Fidelity* can also claim a truly international readership, having been translated into at least fifteen languages to date.

With regard to criticism, periodicals and newspapers have published a number of overviews of Hornby's works in recent years. Notable instances include "Nick Hornby: About a Writer," in the e-journal *Salon* in 1998, and interviews with Francis Leach for the e-zine *Headspace* in November 1998, and with Robert McCrum in the *Observer* in May 2001 following the publication of *How to be Good*. However, critical opinion has not been entirely approving. *About a Boy*, while extremely popular in terms of sales, was considered by various people (myself included) to be a weaker effort than *High Fidelity*. Sarah Kerr's review in *Slate* (May 1998) is admiring of Hornby's writing in general, while arguing convincingly for his second novel being a weaker reiteration of his first. She says: "In all the obvious ways, *About a Boy* feels like a continuation of *High Fidelity*. But where *High Fidelity* argued against too much coolness, the new novel is about the benefits of fitting in."

The broader sweep and "bigger" concerns of *How to be Good* have won Hornby further acclaim and have led to an understanding of certain themes which unite his novels. *High Fidelity* can, for example, now be understood as a novel about much more than the annoying habits of men when seen in the light of later work. For example, Robert McCrum suggests to Hornby that "your role in your work has been as a late twentieth-century dysfunctional Everyman." And yet the tendency still exists to consider Hornby as straddling the fence between comic and literary writing, with the implication that the more straightforwardly comic writing is, the less literary it must be.

SALES

High Fidelity has sold well over a million copies, as has *About a Boy*. This is rather a bald figure, and can be best understood in context of the sales of some similar novels. In terms of the market for so-called "lad" fiction, Hornby has a number of successors and competitors. Novels by two of them, Mike Gayle's debut *My Legendary Girlfriend* (1998) and Tony Parsons's *Man and Boy* (1999) have sold 200,000 copies and 750,000 copies respectively. Parsons's novel has, perhaps like Hornby's, come to be regarded as a "serious" as well as a popular novel. Helen Fielding's *Bridget Jones's Diary*, a comparable success in terms of capturing the *zeitgeist* of the mid-nineties from a female point of view, has itself outstripped *High Fidelity*, selling over four million copies to date. Nevertheless, Hornby's fiction performs extremely well in the market while maintaining credibility more stoically than Fielding's work has managed, factors that resulted in the £2 million contract he signed with Penguin Books in 1999.

How does this performance compare with more "literary" rivals? The 1995 Booker Prize winner, Pat Barker's *The Ghost Road*, is part of her *Regeneration* trilogy about World War I. Together, the three novels have sold 600,000 copies. A Booker Prize win usually boosts sales, so *The Ghost Road* can be expected to have sold a decent share of that figure. Nevertheless, it has probably been only half as successful as *High Fidelity*. Considering that Pat Barker is one of the more well-known authors to win the Booker Prize, this demonstrates the gap between sales of purely "literary" fiction and sales of Hornby's novels: a gap wider than any perceived difference in quality.

HORNBY ON SCREEN

The potential of Hornby's books for adaptation as films has been energetically realized in recent years. *Fever Pitch* was the first to be filmed, starring Colin Firth and with the author himself producing the screenplay. As a first-time screenwriter, Hornby found this an exhilarating experience but one which made him aware of his own inexperience in the field. Consequently, when John Cusack expressed an interest in adapting *High Fidelity* for the big screen, Hornby declined the opportunity to write the screenplay and instead adopted a more consultational role, with Cusack heading a writing and production team and with Stephen Frears as director.

While there are some substantial contextual changes from the original novel (most prominently the change of location from London to Chicago), the adaptation is sensitively and interestingly handled, applauded in most cases for faithfully reproducing the ethos of Hornby's novel. The decision to move the location Stateside was taken by Cusack and his team, who had all grown up in Chicago and "wrote about what they knew," before British director Frears came on board. Frears admits to being skeptical about the change of context until he had read the script, which reassured him that "the human predicament was still there." John Cusack's Rob (given the surname Gordon rather than Fleming) is a suitably flawed hero, behaving badly while also appealing to his audience. It is a film full of male comic peformances, as you might expect, supported by female actresses battling good humoredly against the foibles of men.

The film begins with the words, "What came first? The music or the misery?" spoken as a voice-over by Rob. Then follows the passage in which Rob says "People worry about kids playing with guns, and teenagers watching violent videos; we are scared that some sort of culture of violence will take them over. Nobody worries about kids listening to thousands—literally thousands—of songs about broken hearts and rejection and pain and misery and loss" (p. 27). This sets the framework for the film as one about music and its effect on an individual's everyday life, while allowing the content and tone of the film to slot into the genre of romantic comedy. It is not to do the film an injustice to say that it is a lighter-hearted, more romantic, and more straightforwardly comedic version of Hornby's novel while being impressively faithful to the storyline and, largely, to the dialogue of the text. The areas in which it differs significantly from the novel are: the emphasis on romantic comedy, the details of Rob's musical preferences, and some of the characterizations.

OVERALL TONE

Stephen Frears, in an interview for the film's DVD release, stated: "The more optimistic way Americans live tended to add something to it," and this conveys a great deal of the subtle difference in tone between the original novel, with its frequent and characteristically British gloominess and the breezier atmosphere of the screenplay. Rob's fraught relationship with his parents and suburban background is boiled down to one tragi-comic phone call with his mother in which she finds out that Laura has left him.

Rob begins the film by speaking directly to camera, and this device is continued throughout the film, allowing Cusack to deliver a considerable amount of Rob's inner monologue directly as it appears in the book or with very few alterations. Frears discloses in interview that the decision to have Rob speaking directly to camera was made quickly and early on. After this, he says, it was "easy to get the good bits in," including many of the novel's most appealing monologues. Only one of the monologue scenes is entirely the invention of the producers: that in which Rob compiles a top five list of things he loves about Laura. Clearly, this is a concession to the strictures of romantic comedy, but at least effort was made to maintain the usual style of Rob's thought processes.

Rob's misanthropy in the film is more confident and also quicker to redeem itself. For instance, he flatly refuses the offers of compilation tapes from Dick, whereas in the novel he accepts but never plays them. However, a remark like "I've read books like *The Unbearable Lightness of Being*, and I think I understood them—they were about girls, right?" (p. 29), is followed by a swift "Just kidding" in the film to demonstrate that Rob will eventually be revealed as misguided and willing to overtly mock his own shortcomings, where in the original text he is deliberately shallow and genuinely cynical.

MUSIC—"EVERYONE'S AN EXPERT"

The scriptwriting team also chose the music for *High Fidelity* the film; Cusack wryly remarked in an interview about the quarrels that resulted, that "everyone's an expert." Barry's infamous Monday morning compilation tape replaces Dick's choice of Belle and Sebastian, giving a more well-known (though still minority) and distinctly British flavor to Dick's own musical tastes. Rob's remark about *The Unbearable Lightness of Being* is followed by "However, my all-time favorite book is still Johnny Cash's autobiography, *Cash by Johnny Cash*," a musical signpost we might not have expected from the Rob in the novel.

Generally speaking, the film's concern is to portray Rob as an obsessive music fan without this obsession being too confined or narrow in its choices of listening matter. While favorites from the novel, such as The Clash, Marvin Gaye, and Bruce Springsteen are name checked (Springsteen even makes a cameo appearance), Championship Vinyl also accommodates more contemporary acts on the fringes of the rock/pop genre, such as Stereolab. The producers are none too concerned about precisely where to date this musical landscape. Frears comments that the film is about "a guy obsessed by music from the past," but the film actually broadens Rob's fixations into a firm belief in the superiority of traditional rock and soul music, which coexists with a tolerance and even interest in more recent music in the interests of pleasing browsers in the store.

Rob's anger at other people's musical tastes, such an important part of his characterization in the novel, is offloaded in the film onto the "eccentrics" Dick and Barry, reducing his role as fellow guardian of musical taste to one of controlling their (particularly Barry's) excesses of intolerance. This is clearly an effort to make Rob a more rounded character, one whose oddities can be redeemed by the love of a good woman rather than the need to do any particularly deep thinking about his own mind and the way he allows it to work. Cusack remarks that "Rob's the healthy one of the trio . . . he's sort of, like, you know, ballast." This statement echoes Rob's own need, as articulated in the text, for "ballast," in his own life, something he feels he is unable to generate or hold on to. The fact that he, relative to the characters around him, represents "ballast" in the film shows something of the shift in his character, from someone who loses control completely before taking a second chance to use it more wisely, to a man whose erring from the path of true love is more easily corrected and more willingly indulged.

Finally, Barry's capitulation in terms of giving the audience what they want, rather than the threatened radical stance of Sonic Death Monkey, is more endearing in the film. A particularly nice touch is their performance of "Let's Get It On," one of the songs Laura and Rob agree on as a classic, as the play-out of the film. I would argue that this is an improvement on the novel. It provides a moment where compromise can evoke unity, rather than the grudging concession to populism that Barry makes in the original text.

HORNBY'S ONSCREEN FUTURE

Cusack's adaptation of *High Fidelity* earned both general appreciation and a highly respectable box office showing, making $27 million in the United States and around £5 million in the UK. The run of Hornby adaptations is set to continue: Robert De Niro's Tribeca Productions film company paid £2 million for the rights to produce *About a Boy*, and signed up Hugh Grant, fresh from his triumph in *Bridget Jones's Diary*, to play the lead. *About a Boy* will be released in 2002, and on the basis of previous form, an agreement to adapt *How To Be Good* for film is unlikely to be far behind.

5

Further Reading and Discussion Questions

DISCUSSION QUESTIONS

1. "So close is the tone [of *High Fidelity*] to that of *Fever Pitch* that the reader's instinct is to accept the intimacy of the voice, allowing it to obliterate the distinction between fact and fiction" (Charles Hopkinson). Is this true? If so, what effect does it have on your reading of the novel?
2. "In writing about this very contemporary type, Hornby refuses the false choice between male backlash and fiction that is bloodlessly P.C." (Rob Nixon). Can these polarized options of "male backlash" and "bloodlessly P.C." be found in the novel? Examine the implications of this statement.
3. "Write down the worst four things you've done to your partner—OK, who's the arsehole now?" (p. 80). What effect does being addressed directly by Rob have on you as a reader? If you have seen the film adaptation, consider the effect of John Cusack's speeches direct to camera. Do you prefer the effect in the film or the book?

4. How "universal" a novel is *High Fidelity*? Discuss the factors that might enhance or diminish a reader's understanding of the book, such as nationality and gender.
5. How justified is Rob in blaming pop music for the unhappy lives of its fans?
6. Does Rob actually achieve maturity at the end of the novel? Discuss the extent to which his reinvention of himself as a mature, responsible adult is convincing to the reader.
7. How true is it that obsessions, like Rob's for pop music, are a particularly masculine indulgence?
8. Discuss the evidence presented in *High Fidelity* that masculine and feminine qualities are either biologically inherent or culturally imposed.
9. "Fulfilling work is a great thing at times like these. What am I supposed to do? Go and unlock the shop and walk around it?" (p. 111). Examine the ways in which work can be fulfilling in *High Fidelity*.
10. "She's like this sometimes, Liz. She's OK, but, you know, she's one of those paranoid feminists who see evil in everything you say" (p. 156). How are women and feminism portrayed in *High Fidelity*? What evidence is there for Rob's opinion of Liz, and vice versa?

CRITICAL EXERCISES

1. Many of Rob's opinions on subjects like male/female relationships are presented as an appeal to "common sense," as knowledge that either cannot be denied or can be empirically (at least by him) proven. Take a sample of Rob's statements—such as the

passage where he claims that at the age women want foreplay, men donot (pp. 16–17). Carry out a search of the media to see what statistics can be found to support or refute this theory. Then, note instances where the media suggests, by inference or stated opinion, that this situation is true or false. Examine what sources provide a view of these issues, how they approach the subject, and critically appraise how much influence they have on both "public opinion," and conventional wisdom.

2. Examine the presentation of women's lives and feminism in *High Fidelity*. Compare this presentation with either a) that in a novel from the same period also written by a man, e.g. Tony Parson or Martin Amis, or b) a contemporary novel written by a woman, such as Helen Fielding.
3. The trend of nineties "confessional fiction" means that novels like *High Fidelity* are often considered to be almost documentary. Choose a section of the novel and compare it to a section from a non-fiction, autobiographical text. What stylistic features of they have in common? How, if at all, can one tell which is "real" and which fictional? What effect does this have on the way we read either text?
4. Consider Laura's statement on McDonalds and Burger King, "I know there's a difference, but can anybody be bothered to work out what it is?" Examine the importance of consumer choice like this. Under what circumstances might these choices be important?
5. Rewrite a section of the novel in the third person, i.e, "Rob mused on," instead of "I thought." This should highlight the way in which the distinctive first-person voice operates in the novel. What has been gained, or lost, in the new version?
6. Compile a soundtrack to your own life—list tracks that you have particularly liked, that are associated with particular events, that

hold memories for you. How far does this overlaps with your usual musical preferences? How powerful a role does music play in your life? What is "good" music, by today's standards, and how much do those standards differ from yours, or Rob's?

FURTHER READING

Works by Nick Hornby

Fever Pitch (1992)

This was the book which made Hornby's name. It is partly autobiography, partly a history of football (and Arsenal Football Club in particular) from 1968 until 1989. Charting Hornby's support of the club from the point where his father began taking him to matches, until the year in which they won the League Championship and FA Cup "double," it serves as both a personal history and an examination of the cultural and social experience of being a football fan.

Even for readers who know nothing about football, *Fever Pitch* is likely to be of interest. One review described it as "a sophisticated study of obsession, families, masculinity, class, identity, growing up, loyalty, depression and joy," which summarizes neatly the aspects of it which may interest any reader, and which students of Hornby's work will recognize as characteristic. It goes beyond being a sports book to chronicle a childhood shaped by the cultural mores of late-Sixties and early Seventies suburbia. Descriptions of how a broken family operated, at a time when access visits from divorced parents were an unusual occurrence, capture glimpses of this lifestyle: "The three of us would drive to a neighbouring town, or one of the airport hotels, and Gill and I would eat steak or chicken, one or the other, in more or less complete silence, while Dad watched" (p. 16). It also gives, in retrospect, considerable insights into the development of social groups and cultural trends which came to light in the UK during the 1990s.

About A Boy (1998)

This is Hornby's second novel, which in many ways treads ground familiar to readers of *High Fidelity*. It also revisits the strong focus on the parent-child relationship which dominated *Fever Pitch*. The protagonist, Will Freeman, seems at first to be a version of Rob Fleming advanced even further into inertia. A thirtysomething Londoner who has never had a job because he lives off his father's songwriting royalties, he spends his days saturated in pop culture until meeting Marcus, a twelve-year-old who lives with his folk-music-loving, vegetarian single mother. Marcus and Will proceed to influence one another to the extent that they adopt behaviors more appropriate to the other's respective stage in life. The novel's resolution seems slightly artificial (more so, to my mind, than the appropriately bittersweet ending to *High Fidelity*) but contains, as did the earlier novel, some wonderfully comic dialogue and perceptive characterization.

The novel also pushes further the question of why one needs an occupation in life. Will manages rather well without one—his utter lack of personal relationships being his real downfall. However, Will is too light a character to bear the weight of this investigation; *About a Boy* is very much an ensemble piece, examining relations between the (deliberately) half-formed personalities of its characters, rather than penetrating the depth of individual, painful memories, as happens in *High Fidelity*. The ending may be overly anxious to assure us that things turn out well, but the body of the narrative gives an often bleak insight into single parenthood and lonely childhood in a big city, tormented by the style conscious youth culture which governs school life. As with his previous books, Hornby renders a certain slice of life—the dysfunctional family in London in the early 1990s—with convincing realism and warmth. It moves away from previous concerns with the obsessive behavior of individuals to an insistence that such behaviors have to be slotted into the context of some kind of community, if an unexpected and bizarre one.

Speaking with the Angel (2000)

This collection of short stories was put together by Hornby to raise money for Treehouse, the organization supporting autistic children which he co-founded. Conveniently, it offers an opportunity to be a charitable consumer (£1 from every copy sold goes to Treehouse) and to access samples of the work of many well-known and well-regarded writers of recent years, including stories by Robert Harris, Roddy Doyle, Irvine Welsh, Helen Fielding, and Dave Eggers. It provides a good background to the kind of fiction that is contemporary with Hornby's. His own story, "Nipplejesus," is an explicit discussion of the importance of art, the values that might be found in it being popular or controversial, and the judgements of people who, stereotypically, would have no interest in the avant-garde: in this instance, a former bouncer who takes a job in an art gallery. The story could be seen as a sly defense of the views of the "ordinary," anti-intellectual viewer against art which is outrageous and anti-realistic merely for the purpose of shocking. It is Hornby's revenge, perhaps, on those who prefer their fiction to be *avant-garde*.

How To Be Good (2001)

This, Hornby's third novel, is definitely his most challenging work yet. It was received with new respect and was considered as a serious contender for the Booker Prize shortlist (though it was not, finally, included). It follows the ethical struggles of Katie Carr, a doctor who believes herself fallible but still morally superior to her husband David—who is a cynical newspaper columnist until he undergoes a spiritual conversion and begins a crusade to rehabilitate homeless youths and share the Carrs' middle-class prosperity with them. Even this subject is treated with Hornby's usual wry humor, and there are moments of real comedy in the excruciating confrontations between the new, saintly David and the people who expect him to be his old bitter self. Particularly good scenes occur when he attempts to give the family's Sunday dinner away to the homeless and when he tells an old sparring partner that they must understand Monica Lewinsky's pain and not joke about her. Middle of the road liberalism is Hornby's subject here—one critic described the novel as a story told from the "point of view of the camel who couldn't go through the eye of the needle." It received a flurry of attention because of the supposedly controversial idea of Hornby writing from a woman's perspective, but its reception proves that Hornby is ready to forge a reputation which goes beyond being "the master of the male confessional."

In addition to the above books, Hornby has edited and contributed to a number of other books, mainly on football, and occasionally music, which hold more interest for enthusiasts of those subjects than for the general reader. Nevertheless, if readers want to acquire a comprehensive Hornby collection, there are certainly non-fiction items to be added to the above list of fiction.

Furthermore, Hornby shows signs of wanting to extend his original fictional world into one which networks across his series of fictional North London communities, in reintroducing, albeit briefly, elements of *High Fidelity* into later novels. In *About a Boy*, Will is "browsing in a record shop, Championship Vinyl," when he spies his first single-mother girlfriend; and in *How to be Good*, Katie moves into a bedsit which is part of a converted house, where one resident, Dick, is clearly the Dick who passes his days at Championship Vinyl. It will be interesting to see if these references to *High Fidelity* and its characters become a Hitchcock-like regular presence in Hornby's future fictions.

Works by other novelists

Anne Tyler, The Accidental Tourist *(1985),* Breathing Lessons *(1988)*

As well as being Hornby's favorite novelist, Tyler's work is immensely popular and critically well regarded. She published her first novel in 1964 and has written prolifically ever since. Her novels are usually narratives of family crisis, misunderstanding and reconciliation, told with insight and humor, and set in Baltimore, where she has lived for many years. Perhaps her best-known and most accessible novel is *The Accidental Tourist,* which was adapted for film and tells the story of how Macon Leary, a travel writer obsessed by routine, is forced to change his life after the death of his son. *Breathing Lessons,* which won a Pulitzer Prize, examines the marriage of Maggie and Ira Moran and their relationships with family and friends. Either would be a good introduction to Tyler's work.

Charles Dickens, David Copperfield *(1850),* Great Expectations *(1861)*

Dickens's novels demonstrate the template from which Hornby is working in writing realist novels and social comedies rooted firmly in the London landscape. *David Copperfield* and *Great Expectations* are both classics in their portrayals of confused young men looking for meaning in life and their way through the world. Against this background, Hornby's novels can be seen as part of a tradition that was established well before the New Lad was ever invented.

Fictions of masculinity

High Fidelity heralded a rash of novels about end-of-the-century masculinity and about the delayed onset of maturity for characters similar to Rob Fleming. Some interesting examples of the genre, varying in popularity and literariness, by British writers are:

Mike Gayle: *My Legendary Girlfriend* (1998) and *Mr. Commitment* (1999)

John McCabe: *Stickleback* (1999)

Tony Parsons: *Man and Boy* (1999)

Mark Barrowcliffe: *Girlfriend 44* (2000)

Tim Lott: *White City Blue* (1999)

Damian Lanigan: *Stretch, 29* (2001)

Helen Fielding, Bridget Jones's Diary *(1996)*

This novel is often thought of as the female equivalent to *High Fidelity*. Fielding's influence on popular culture and perceptions of femininity and gender relations can be compared to the impact Hornby's work has had over the last few years. Her heroine, the "singleton," thirtysomething, Chardonnay-swilling, chain-smoking Bridget, triggered interest in the "post-feminist" heroine attempting to construct a meaningful life as a single woman with a career, while also pursuing a pre-feminist path of anxiety over her appearance and trying to catch a man. Bridget's woes struck a chord with millions of readers around the world with the result that Fielding's novel is regarded as defining the dilemma of the 1990s woman, while also receiving criticism from some feminists for apparently giving credence to regressive ideas about women's frivolity and dependence on male attention. Fielding herself has always stated that the *Diary* is a comic novel and it can certainly be read as an important contribution to the fictional landscape of the period, without being awarded the status of a documentary report. As a fiction which describes specifically feminine experiences and traits, it provides a very useful gender counterpart to *High Fidelity* and the London scene described there.

Internet sites

Penguin have an official Nick Hornby website, which is at *www.penguin.co.uk/static/packages/uk/articles/hornby* and provides a list of Hornby's works with reviewers' comments, interview material, and commentary from Hornby himself, and the facility to send comments to the author.

Amazon's sites can be searched for information on works by Hornby. These pages provide useful information such as links to other books which have also been purchased by Hornby's readers, customer reviews, and sales rankings for the novels.

Yahoo! hosts a Nick Hornby reading group, which can be found at *http://dir.groups.yahoo.com/dir/Entertainment Arts/Humanities/ Books and Writing/Genres/Literary Fiction/Authors/Hornby, Nick* where readers can post messages and join in discussion about Hornby and his work.

The Voice of the Shuttle website at *http://vos.ucsb.edu/index-netscape.asp* is one of the most comprehensive internet guides to literature and cultural studies, giving articles, questions, and criticism on a bewildering variety of categories of writing. There is little academic criticism on Hornby currently available, but readers who want to research areas such as "Contemporary British Fiction," or "The Modern American Novel," which are pertinent to Hornby's work, will certainly find that it has a lot to offer.

Bibliography

Works by Nick Hornby:

Fever Pitch, 1992 (London: Indigo, 1996)
High Fidelity, 1995 (London: Indigo, 1996)
About a Boy, 1998 (London: Indigo, 1999)
Speaking with the Angel (ed. and introd. by Hornby), 2000, (London: Penguin, 2000)
How to be Good, 2001 (London: Penguin, 2001)

Interviews with Nick Hornby:

Steffan Chirazi, *Salon*, 31 March 2000
Francis Leach, *Headspace*, November 1998.
Robert McCrum, *The Observer*, 27 May 2001.

Reviews of *High Fidelity*:

Mick Brown, *The Independent*, 1 April 1995.
Harry Enfield, *The Independent On Sunday*, 18 June 1995.
John Harvey, *San Francisco Chronicle*, 6 November 1995.
Charles Hopkinson, *The Independent On Sunday*, 9 April 1995.

David Horspool, *Times Literary Supplement*, 31 March 1995.
Michelle Huneven, *Los Angeles Times*, 24 December 1995.
Sarah Kerr, *Slate*, May 1998
Suzanne Moore, *The Guardian*, 28 March 1995.
Rob Nixon, *The New Yorker*, 11 September 1995.

Other works

Chris Baldick, (ed.), *The Concise Oxford Dictionary of Literary Terms* (Oxford and New York: Oxford University Press, 1992)

Jerome Buckley, *Seasons of Youth: the bildungsroman from Dickens to Golding* (Cambridge, Mass.: Harvard University Press, 1974)

Ian Miles, 'Masculinity and its discontents', in *Futures: the journal of forecasting and planning*, February 1989, 21:1, pp. 47–59.

Franco Moretti, *The Way of the World: the* Bildungsroman *in European culture* (London: Verso, 1987)

Lynne Segal, *Slow Motion: Changing Masculinities, Changing Men* (London: Virago, revised edition 1997; first published 1990).

Dominic Strinati, *An Introduction to Theories of Popular Culture* (London and New York: Routledge, 1997).